Over 55 Is Not Illegal

Books by Frances Tenenbaum

Gardening with Wild Flowers
Nothing Grows for You?
Plants from Nine to Five
Over 55 Is *Not* Illegal

Over 55 Is *Not* Illegal

A Resource Book for Active Older People

Frances Tenenbaum

Houghton Mifflin Company   Boston   1979

Library of Congress Cataloging in Publication Data

Tenenbaum, Frances.
    Over 55 is not illegal.

    1. Aged — United States — Services for — Directories.
2. Aged — United States — Services for — Handbooks,
manuals, etc. 3. Age and employment — United States —
Handbooks, manuals, etc. 4. Education for the aged —
United States — Handbooks, manuals, etc. 5. Aged —
United States — Recreation — Handbooks, manuals, etc.
6. Middle age. I. Title.
HV1457.T45   362.6′0973   78-27657
ISBN 0-395-27595-4

Printed in the United States of America

M 10 9 8 7 6 5 4 3 2 1

Drawings by Jane Tenenbaum

Photo on page 95, © Karen Preuss, from *Life Time, A New Image of Aging,*
published by Unity Press, Santa Cruz, California, 1978

For Laya Wiesner

Acknowledgments

A resource book like this one could not possibly be written without the help of hundreds of people who were kind enough to answer questions, fill out questionnaires, suggest new sources, lend pictures, and offer good advice. I am grateful to all of them, with special thanks to Mary Power, librarian for the American Association of Retired Persons. The book *literally* could not have been written without Miriam Brooks, who telephoned and typed and filed and generally kept me afloat in a high sea of paper. Most of all, thanks to Austin Olney of Houghton Mifflin, who matched my enthusiasm and encouraged me in what has turned out to be a fascinating project of discovery.

Contents

Introduction

If you are 55 years old, one third of your life is before you. One of the unrecognized facts of life in the last quarter of the twentieth century is that longevity has come of age. At 55, we can statistically look forward to a span of years longer than childhood and adolescence combined.

For those of us who spent our childhoods growing up and our young adulthoods climbing career ladders and raising families—confident that middle age would always remain ten years away—planning for our older age simply was not on the agenda. The somewhat vague assumption that it would represent the leisure to do all those (usually unnamed) things we didn't have time for in youth did not take into consideration whether these would be satisfying projects for twenty or thirty years.

If we didn't plan for our own longevity, our institutions didn't either—youth-oriented society is more than a phrase. And when finally it became clear that there were old people in the land of the young, the attention quite rightly was on services to the poor, the frail, and the sick; on the very serious problems of poverty, housing, and health care that affect older people out of all proportion to their numbers. Ironically, however, this emphasis on problems has created a wildly distorted picture of aging, which, as the National Council on the Aging points out, may be the biggest problem of all.

Because suddenly, although most of us still don't know it, there is something new in America—a new generation, many millions in number, who may or may not be retired from work, but have no intention of retiring from full participation in a lively life. With years before them, they are no longer willing to pass time but are determined to spend it productively. Many of this new older generation have found resources on their own, but many more do not know what is available—and for good reason, since most of the exciting and creative opportunities designed specifically to attract or use the talents of older people are simply too new to be well known. Very few of the programs you will find in this book were in existence even a few years ago. Every day, it seems, some college or organization or individual sets up some innovative program somewhere in the country.

Many of these, along with all the national programs, appear in the pages that follow. Unfortunately, there is no way to include every one. For one thing, no one knows them all, and for that reason I would be interested to learn about any that don't appear here.

My original intention for this book was simply to collect the names and addresses and descriptions of as many programs in education, volunteering, work, and recreation designed specifically for older people as I could uncover. I found many more and in much greater variety than I could have imagined, but along the way my never wholly quiescent journalistic instincts took me farther afield and I discovered a story about aging in America that has not been told, at least in one place.

I learned that our picture of aging is outdated, distorted, and often wholly inaccurate. Our "facts" are largely myths, and these myths have allowed us to create a stereotyped image of an older person as an appendage to society, not a full participating member. Even older people who do not recognize themselves in the stereotypes accept them as true for *others;* assuming themselves to be the exceptions, they accept the opinions of an ageist society.

I learned about ageism—a concept so new that the word has not yet joined racism and sexism in my modern dictionary—how it manifests itself, how it can impede everything you try to do, how some older people are trying to combat it, and how you can join the fight.

In the year 2020, when the postwar babies come of age, one in every four Americans will be over 65. This is a truly staggering fact and one that has implications for everyone, old as well as young, right now. For one thing, in case you're accustomed to thinking of older people as has-beens, you ought to see them as new pioneers—they are the first generation of their kind.

The size of the present older population and the projections for the future have spurred interest in research on aging and the study of aging. The National Institute on Aging, the newest of the National Institutes of Health, was created only in 1974; it is already clearing away the underbrush of mythology that has distorted our picture of aging.

Gerontology, the scientific study of aging, is perhaps the youngest academic discipline; it is certainly the fastest-growing one. Colleges all over the country are offering courses in gerontology. Because these courses are attracting not only young students but people working in the field and older people themselves, descriptions of these programs appear in this book.

But I also learned that we do not have to wait for future knowledge to improve our lives today. Drugs and alcohol are metabolized differently in older people; some medications prescribed to alleviate a specific condition cause reactions that are then misdiagnosed as "age" and therefore ignored. Diet and exercise can enhance the quality of an older person's life, and there are even ways to improve memory. This kind of information, because it is a practical, positive personal resource, is included in this book too.

So a major resource here is knowledge. Clearly, you can't live a full late-life in today's world if your picture of that world is out of date. Even more obvious—or it ought to be—is that people who work with older people should know who they really are, not who they were ten years ago (if ever). To make the most of your life, you need to be free of the limitations of the past and aware of the opportunities of the present. I hope you will find a world of opportunities in this book.

Part I

The New Breed of Older People

CHAPTER 1

Growing Older—Facts, Myths, and Stereotypes

Facts and Figures

Older people are the fastest growing minority in this country. Given the alternative, this is the one minority everyone hopes someday to join. Yet simply to say that America is growing older does not convey the scope and speed of the phenomenon. Statistics, in this case, tell the story better than words.

One in every nine Americans is over 65. One in every seven is over 60. One in every five is over 55. In just seven years, between 1970 and 1977, while the general population increased by 5 percent, the over-65 population jumped by *18* percent. The fastest growing group was the over-85-year-olds.

Proportion of Population Aged 65+: 1976

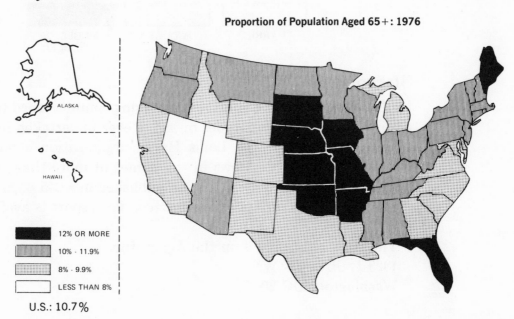

ALASKA

HAWAII

12% OR MORE

10% - 11.9%

8% - 9.9%

LESS THAN 8%

U.S.: 10.7%

Every day, the 65-plus population increases by 1500 persons. If birth and death rates remain the same, the older population will peak in the year 2020, when the postwar babies join its ranks. At that time, *one out of every four* Americans will be over 65.

If you are 35 years old today and a man, the chances are eight in ten that you will live to be at least 60. If you are a woman, your chances are nine in ten. And if you are 65 today and a man, your life expectancy is fourteen years. If you are a woman, eighteen years.

If you are 55, one third of your life is before you.

Most older men (79 percent) are married. Most older women (53 percent) are widows. There are five and a half times as many widows as widowers.

With so many older people amongst us, we presumably should know a lot about them. When we get beyond the statistics, though, it turns out that most of our facts are myths and our perceptions about older people are based on stereotypes not founded in reality.

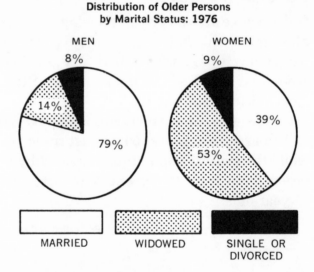

Distribution of Older Persons
by Marital Status: 1976

Stereotypes

In 1975, the National Council on the Aging commissioned the most extensive study on the attitudes on aging ever undertaken in this country. Interviewers for the Louis Harris organization conducted 6000 hours of in-depth interviews in the homes of more than 4000 people. The results of that study have been published in a 245-page report, *The Myth and Reality of Aging in America*. The report is available for $9 from:

The National Council on the Aging, Inc.
1828 L Street, N.W.
Washington, DC 20036

Much of what we know about how people—old and young—perceive the experience of aging is the result of that study.

Asked what were "the best things about old age," both the 18–64 and the over-65 groups gave high marks to "having more leisure." Interestingly, though, the younger people mentioned it more often than those who actually had more time for leisure.

But it is on the reverse side of the coin that the really significant discrepancies appear between the actuality of old age and the public's perception of it.

When asked to volunteer what they considered the worst things about being over 65, poor health, followed by loneliness, financial problems, lack of independence, being neglected or rejected by the young, and boredom were cited by both groups. Yet, in virtually every case the younger group vastly overstated the problems when compared to how people over 65 experienced them personally. As an example of the distorted view that the public has of what it is like to get old, the Harris survey points out these "enormous" discrepancies between the perception and the reality:

Fifty percent of the public felt "fear of crime" to be a serious problem of the old, but only 23 percent of the people over 65 found it to be a problem.

Fifty-one percent of the public thought poor health was a serious problem for older people, but only 21 percent of the older people found that it was.

While 62 percent of the public expected that old age meant "not having enough money to live on," only 15 percent of the older group experienced it as a serious personal problem. The discrepancies were similar for inadequate medical care, loneliness, and other problems. As a final example of the gap between the perception and the reality of aging, while 54 percent of the general public thought "not feeling needed" would be a serious problem, only 7 percent of the over-65 group agreed that it was.

There's more behind these answers than statistics. The questions above, for the older group, were directed to the problems they *personally* had. But when people over 65 were asked what problems they felt old people *in general* had, their replies very much matched those of the 18–64 sample. In other words, each person considered himself or herself an exception. Or, as the Harris pollsters put it, old people, like the young, have bought the negative images of old age.

One can conclude that, while serious problems of not enough money, fear of crime, poor health, loneliness, inadequate medical care, and getting where they want to go do indeed exist among certain minorities of older people, they are by no means as all-pervasive as the public thinks. Nor should having a problem be confused with being a problem.

Such generalizations about the elderly as an economically and socially deprived group can do the old a disservice, for they confront older people with a society who sees them merely as a problem and not a part of the solution to many of society's problems. As a result, older people are not likely to find themselves the recipients of opportunities to pitch in and help solve the problems that affect our society as a whole.

Putting an exclusive emphasis on the problems of old age, the Harris report adds, "can do the young a disservice too since these reminders of what life will be like for them may tempt them to turn their heads away from the elderly and focus on a youth-oriented society."

To call the typical picture of older Americans a caricature, as the National Council on the Aging does, is not to deny the fact that there are millions of older people who live lives of poverty and deprivation, vastly out of proportion to their numbers. However, "the wildly distorted image of old age may be its biggest problem of all. The older population is not as a whole sick and frail, or poor, or forgotten residents of institutions, or consumed with unproductive leisure. Such labels do not accurately describe either most older people or the great variety of energy and resources which exist within today's aged population."

Dr. Robert N. Butler, Director of the National Institute on Aging and author of the Pulitzer-Prize-winning book, *Why Survive? Being Old in America,* says that there is a greater diversity both physiologically and in terms of personality in the oldest age group than in any other.

> It is becoming more common to find retired people in their sixties and seventies who have living parents in their eighties and nineties. Sometimes it is the 80-year-old who is taking care of the 60-year-old! Chronological age is an inaccurate measure of how old one is because aging ... occurs unevenly—one may be at different "ages" at one and the same time in terms of mental capacity, physical health, endurance, creativity, and emotions. Society has arbitrarily chosen ages 60–65 as the beginning of late life ... This social definition has had its legitimate uses as well as its abuses. Not everyone is ready to retire at 60 or 65. Older people do not appreciate the "social" definition of old age encroaching into every corner of their lives, rigidly stamping them with a ... label.

Since the Harris survey found that the public's perception of older people was of a group beset by problems, these next findings are not surprising. Asked to judge old age on a list of attributes generally associated with productive, active, and effective individuals, "most people over 65" received high marks from the general public in two areas only—"warm and friendly" and "wise from experience."

"Seen as nice old folks who have benefited from the trials and tribulations of life, most people over 65 are not viewed, however, as very active, efficient, or alert people." Only 35 percent considered them "very good at getting things done," 29 percent, "very bright and alert," and 21 percent, "very open-minded and adaptable."

(I must say I have some argument with this section of the Harris poll. By using the word "very," I think they may have skewed the results somewhat. I wonder how many of the respondents would have called "most people" of any age "very" open-minded and adaptable. However, even if you added a few percentage points, the public image of people over 65 remains the same.)

With one exception, the over-65 group had a slightly better image of itself than did the younger group, but it wasn't by much and they, too, "have bought the stereotypes of older people as unalert, closed-minded, unproductive members of society." The one exception was "warm and friendly." Eighty-two percent of the younger group thought of older people in that way but only 25 percent of the over-65 sample thought their contemporaries could be described as "warm and friendly."

Unhealthy Myths

"Old People Can't Learn"

Not only can old people learn, but, as the chapter on education indicates, "learning" is one of the things they are doing best and enjoying most.

Still, the myth remains and the cliché that you can't teach an old dog new tricks is often given pseudoscientific validity by the "fact" of irreversible loss of brain cells. While scientists have long pointed out that the brain has more cells than it can use in a lifetime, the loss theory itself is now being questioned.

In the January–February 1978 issue of *American Scientist,* Marian C. Diamond, Professor of Anatomy at the University of California at Berkeley, writes that the higher centers of mammalian brains do not lose large numbers of nerve cells from maturity to old age. Professor Diamond says that studies by many scientists indicate that "there is good evidence that drastic structural changes do not occur in the mammalian brain with aging" if there is a stimulating environment.

Dr. Butler adds that "longitudinal studies—those that follow the same people over a long period of time—clearly show that the intellectual abilities of healthy people grow greater through the years, not less." And the National Council on the Aging reports that vocabulary and conceptual skills often grow after 60.

Forgetfulness and a decline in speed of response are probably the indicators behind the myth that old people cannot learn. There is some decline in speed of response but, as far as learning goes, this is offset by experience and maturity. It is of no particular consequence unless you are in a race—unless other people get impatient and make you think it is. Many older people are no more forgetful than the young. The difference is that old people worry about forgetfulness, and anxiety and depression lead to increased forgetfulness.

Dr. Stephen H. Zarit, director of a new memory clinic at the Andrus Gerontology Center of the University of Southern California, has been studying memory in healthy older people and has found that age does not affect memory to a significant degree. "What happens is that when they forget something, many older people say, 'I must be getting old.' The younger person who does the same thing shrugs and ignores it."

The fact remains that many older people *do* become forgetful—or there wouldn't be memory clinics. Scientists at the National Institute on Aging have found that mnemonics can be quite helpful in helping older people store and retrieve information. Mnemonics is a classic memory-improvement technique that involves associating items to be learned with stops on an imaginary journey.

Memory clinics are a relatively new concept, but there are a few that are open to the public. Colleges and universities also offer classes that teach techniques for memory retention—look for them in the adult education or extension catalogues. Dr. Zarit says there are several techniques that are effective and that by exercising the mind, by testing it, and using it more, "we are generally more able to take in information and remember it." He recommends the *Memory Book* by Harry Lorayne and Jerry Lucas. It is often used in memory classes and contains several chapters that help people remember names and faces, shopping lists, and vocabulary, and how to avoid absent-mindedness.

Failing memory is embarrassing and can contribute to problems in daily living, but the main reason it is so worrying is because of its association with one of the most fallacious—and most disturbing—myths of aging, senility.

"Senility"

"Going out of your head, losing your memory, or becoming 'senile' is statistically an unlikely misfortune," writes gerontologist Alex Comfort in his book, *A Good Age*. "The word 'senile' is less a diagnosis than a term of abuse."

In actuality, about 1 percent of all people become senile in old age, a far smaller percentage than become mentally ill at younger ages.

"To begin with," writes Dr. Butler, " 'senility' is not, properly speaking, a medical diagnosis at all but a wastebasket term for a range of symptoms that, minimally, includes some memory impairment or forgetfulness, difficulty in attention and concentration, decline in general intellectual grasp and ability, and reduction in emotional responsiveness to others. This condition, as studies at the National Institutes of Health and elsewhere have made clear, is not an inevitable consequence of age *per se*. Rather, it is a reflection of any of a variety of different problems."

At a rough guess, Dr. Butler estimates that perhaps one million, or one of every twenty-three older Americans "may have some form of intellectual dysfunction that might get labeled 'senility.' " He estimates that 50 percent of these cases are reversible.

True senility is an organic brain disease called senile dementia. The other reversible (if understood and caught) "senilities" are what Dr. Leslie S. Libow, Medical Director of the Jewish Institute for Geriatric Care on Long Island, calls "pseudosenilities." And for these, says Dr. Butler, there are a "hundred" causes. They include viral infections, alcohol and medications (see chapter 9), depression, and simple malnutrition.

Dr. Libow advises that if the family doctor diagnoses senility, a second opinion should be sought from a neurologist, a psychiatrist specializing in the problems of elderly people, or a geriatrician. That prescription is easier to give than to follow—there are very few geropsychiatrists (Dr. Butler is one) or geriatricians in this country. If your own doctor can't suggest a specialist, call your medical society or the teaching hospital in your community.

Alex Comfort's advice on doctors is blunter: "If you find someone who thinks that in the natural order you have to be infirm, crazy, impotent or the like, by virtue of chronological age, change doctors."

The Myth of "Disengagement"

This term, which Dr. Comfort attributes to "Disneyland sociology," describes the theory that we naturally "pull up tent pegs" as we age. "In our culture," says Comfort, "it is often, alas, sludge language for being ejected, excluded, or demeaned," an attribute "wished on the old to plaster our guilt and provide a piece of jargon to excuse our conduct." Comfort adds, "at any age you can opt out from what you have been doing, often because it is seen not to be worthwhile."

"Old People Are Abandoned by Their Families"

The corollary to this myth is the one that pictures families dumping their older members into nursing homes. In truth, Dr. Butler says, "fully half of the people in nursing homes have no families at all. As for those who do, in Dr. Butler's experience, "this decision is made only after the family makes incredible efforts to keep the relative at home."

In the Louis Harris survey, as we have seen, loneliness and "not being needed" were assumed by the younger age group to be far greater problems than the over-65 group actually found them to be. According to a study by Dr. Ethel Shanas, 80 percent of people over 65 live with someone else; 75 percent say they are "not often alone," and 86 percent see one or two relatives a week. In actual numbers, less than 4 percent of all people over 65 live in institutions.

The Trouble with Stereotypes

As all minorities or oppressed peoples know, accepting the stereotypes of society makes them self-fulfilling prophecies. People discriminated against because of racism or sexism have learned that even a good stereotype is damaging—all girls aren't pretty, all boys aren't strong, not all blacks have rhythm, and all old people aren't any more warm and friendly than they all are stubborn and closed-minded.

In studies at the National Institutes of Health, Rorschach inkblot tests were given to American servicemen captured in Korea and, later, to a group of older people. Reports Dr. Butler, "It turned out that those older people who accepted all the stereotypes of age—that you're washed up, you're senile, you're not able to be physically active—reacted to the tests in the same way as those prisoners who had collaborated with the Communists. Those older people who disagreed with what society expected from the aged followed the pattern shown by the prisoners who resisted collaboration."

The trouble with believing and accepting the stereotypes about aging, says Alex Comfort, is that "it prepares people to be victimized at 65 and the rest of us to victimize them until we get there ourselves."

CHAPTER 2

Getting the Message to the Media

The word *ageism* was coined in 1968 by Dr. Robert N. Butler, now Director of the National Institute on Aging, during a stormy opposition to a high-rise housing project for the elderly in Washington. According to Butler, ageism "can be seen as systematic stereotyping of and discrimination against people because they are old, just as racism and sexism accomplish this through skin color and gender ... Ageism allows the younger generation to see older people as different from themselves; thus they can subtly cease to identify with their elders as human beings."

Ageism isn't always subtle. Consider the young instructor at Brandeis University who told a class that old people should not be allowed to vote because, "having no future, they are dangerously far from the consequences of their own political acts, and it makes no sense to allow the vote to someone who is actuarially unlikely to survive and pay the bills."

If the vote is dangerous, imagine an old person being allowed to interpret the whole constitution! Obviously, he would have had justices Holmes, Cardoza, Warren, Frankfurter, and even Brandeis, whose name adorns the university where he made these remarks, kicked off the Supreme Court.

Given the negative images that the public has of the experience of aging, you might expect that the Louis Harris respondents would have placed the blame for these stereotypes squarely on the media, those most powerful image-makers of our society.

Not at all. "The public is not, on the whole, critical of the way the media portray older people." The pollsters go on to explain: "This may mean simply that the media project and maintain the stereotypes the public already holds. With the public at large viewing older people as passive, sedentary types who have lost the open-mindedness, mental alertness, and efficiency of the young, beset with economic problems, poor health and loneliness, it is unlikely that they would criticize the media for portraying older people in the same light."

The Television Image

If the Harris interviewees were not critical, others are. The Media Resource Center of the National Council on the Aging, which sponsored the survey, is using it as the basis for its efforts to inform television and other media of the inaccuracies of the stereotypes they project. The NCOA has opened a Hollywood office that has as its sole purpose lobbying creative people in the television business to improve their portrayal of older people.

According to the *New York Times,* Helyne Landres and Nadine Kearns "offer a hot-line service for TV writers and producers seeking advice on how to treat older characters. The questions put to them sometimes sound as if the callers were seeking guidance on the lifestyles of some fragile, alien culture. One writer said he was thinking of creating a scene calling for a roomful of older folks and wondered whether a doctor would have to be on the set."

Ironically, the *Times* continues, critics of television believe old people are "rebuffed most harshly in television's most trivial area, the game shows."

> Mrs. Landres contends that the game shows, by and large, not only won't use older contestants but won't let older people sit in the front rows of the audience. "I have spoken to every game show producer in town and every one resists. One young woman said, 'Oh, all right, you can bring some of your old people down here and they can watch.' I said, 'They don't want to watch, they want to be the contestants.' She acted as though it were the most idiotic request she ever heard. 'We can't use old people. They're all senile, they talk too much, they're too slow.'"

Some critics aren't much happier about the nice old grandmother of the television commercials. According to Landres, she's about 80, which makes her more likely to be a great- or great-great-grandmother. A real grandmother could be in her late 30s or 40s.

Mrs. Jeanne Schallon, a Los Angeles leader of the Gray Panthers, describes the television grandmothers "in 1890s clothing and silly hats all agog over a sink cleanser" as sickening. To see any woman all agog over a sink cleanser is sickening, as the women's movement often complains, but older women are double victims. Mrs. Schallon continues, "I'm 62, my mind never worked better, but when I take a prescription to the druggist he treats me like an imbecile child. That's the way television has taught him to treat me."

Of course I can't prove that the child who wrote the following essay got all of her impressions from television, but they could hardly have come from real life since the average grandmother of the average third-grader would be in her 50s. Obviously, it was published as cute and appealing, which just goes to confirm what has been said of the willingness of older people to accept negative stereotypes. What is depressing, though, is that this article appeared in a 1978 issue of *Senior Spotlight,* the newsletter of the Minnesota Board on Aging, which should know better.

What Is a Grandmother?
by a Third-Grader

A grandmother is a lady who has no children of her own, so she likes other people's little girls. A grandfather is a man grandmother. He goes for walks with the boys and they talk about fishing and tractors, and like that.

Grandmothers don't have to do anything except be there. They're old, so they shouldn't play hard or run. It is enough if they drive us to the market where the pretend horse is, and have lots of dimes ready. Or, if they take us for walks, they should slow down past things like pretty leaves and caterpillars. They should never say "hurry up."

Usually they are fat, but not too fat to tie kids' shoes. They wear glasses and funny underwear. They can take their teeth and gums off. It is better if they don't typewrite or play cards except with us. They don't have to be smart, only answer questions like why dogs hate cats, and how come God isn't married. They don't talk baby talk like visitors do because it is hard to understand. When they read they don't skip, or mind if it is the same story again.

Everybody should try to have one, especially if you don't have television, because grandmas are the only grownups who've got time.

In our age-stratified society, and with grandparents who may live hundreds or thousands of miles away, most children have little contact with older people. In a study of children's attitudes toward the elderly, professors Richard K. Jantz and Carol Seefeldt of the Department of Early Childhood/Elementary Education of the University of Maryland found that few of the 180 children in the survey could name an older person outside of their own families. Their responses to old people were mixed. While they found them rich, good, clean, and friendly, when it came to physical characteristics, they described them as sick, ugly, and sad. Needless to say, only a small minority of the children had anything positive to say about the prospect of getting old themselves. The Jantz-Seefeldt study is being used as the basis for a curriculum project for elementary school teachers.

Dr. Edward Ansello, Associate Director of the University of Maryland's Center on Aging, found that children learn negative stereotypes of the elderly from their own literature. In 549 books, researchers found only eighty-eight that portrayed older characters in any significant fashion—meaning that a character spoke a line or was clearly identified as being related to the story.

"Children's books are perpetuating this ridiculous myth of the do-nothing, boring, invisible aged person," Dr. Ansello says.

The group that has been most vocal in its criticism of television's view of old age is the Gray Panthers, specifically its Media Watch Committee, headed by Lydia Bragger (see chapter 3). Among the performers and characters the Panthers dislike the most is Johnny Carson's Aunt Blabby who is everything older people resent about their TV image rolled up into one frumpy, unappealing, silly, constantly blabbering old woman. Carson's reaction to the Panther's criticism was summed up in one of his monologues: "The Gray Panthers are a group of older people and they are very militant. They went on a college campus today and gave the sign of the clenched prune."

Carson, says Bragger, "seems to have a hang-up about prunes and old people. I think he's scared to death about getting old."

Although the Gray Panthers haven't succeeded in changing Johnny Carson's mind, they have had some influence with the National Association of Broadcasters, which, after a meeting with the Media Watch Committee, voted to amend the NAB television code to add age to sex, race, color, and creed in its sensitivity guidelines.

Older People Are People Too

This is the title of one of the National Council on the Aging's brochures aimed at changing the media's picture of older people. On television, however, older people simply aren't there. Some years ago, Dr. Robert N. Butler, Director of the National Institute on Aging, served on a panel evaluating how various groups are represented in public television broadcasting. From the programs, he said, "it was possible to conclude that no one grew old or died in America." And that was *public*

"When I am with an older person, I . . ."

In a study of intergenerational differences in attitude toward old people, Professor Anthony J. Traxler, director of the gerontology program of Southern Illinois University at Edwardsville, used as his sample college students (mean age, 24) and their parents (mean age, 52).

To the sentence "When I am with an older person, I . . ." the students most often chose the category mentioning negative feelings, parents the "passive" category. On appearance, students chose the negative descriptive adjective, parents the positive. Students most often completed the sentence "Old people tend to resent . . ." with the words "younger people." Parents chose "intrusion, interference, domination." Seventy-one percent of the parents had good things to say about "most of the older people I have known"; only 48 percent of the students did.

On the whole, students, as opposed to parents, tended to express discomfort and tension when with old people, described them with negative adjectives, and seemed not to value the friendship of an older person. Parents were also less harsh in judging the appearance of old people and expressed attitudes that indicated that old people tended to be neglected and undervalued.

One hypothesis suggested by Dr. Traxler is that old age is seen as undesirable and negative by both students and parents, but because parents are closer to the label "old," the thought of harboring negative attitudes toward old people creates considerable anxiety, and so the older person reverses his negative feelings and expresses positive ones.

broadcasting. Butler has also criticized news reporting for distorting the picture of aging by focusing on instances of old people performing rare feats of strength or endurance, on "cute" news items about late-life love and marriage, or on those creative people who function at a high level "in spite of" age.

Researchers at the University of Pennsylvania's Annenberg School of Communications found that the elderly represented less than 3 percent of the major characters on prime-time network dramatic programming. And, Lydia Bragger adds, most of them are shown as "ugly, toothless, sexless, incontinent, senile, confused, and helpless."

When a television writer asked Helyne Landres whether an 80-year-old man could possibly rob a bank, she replied, "Of course, but please make it clear he was *always* a bank robber." A big objection to the television portrayal of old people is the idea that people suddenly start doing "dumb or terrible things because they are old."

In December 1977, a conference on Images of Old Age in the American Media was convened by the Graduate School of Journalism of Columbia University, the American Jewish Committee, the National Council of Churches, and the Catholic Conference. Representatives from advertising and the media were among those attending. In virtually all of the workshops it was agreed that old people were underrepresented on television or completely absent except as doctors. Even the television people admitted that in family shows the family usually stops at age 50. Nor were there any sensible, strong, virile old people in television commercials—"in advertising everyone thinks people are senile after 50."

Participants in the conference criticized the emphasis on physical and mental illness among the old in the news media. Its excessive preoccupation with nursing homes was said to give a distorted picture because, as previously noted, less than 4 percent of people over 65 are institutionalized and, as the Harris poll indicated, 80 percent consider themselves to be in good health.

Also criticized was the obsession with the aged as poor. In news reporting, "fixed income" has become synonymous with old age.

Studies by the Gray Panthers were cited to show that television constantly depicts old people as victims. As a rule, they appear only briefly and have to have their problems solved by younger people. A report of the conference states: "This image of powerlessness and dependency was thought to be most damaging of all by at least one workshop group where the moderator drew attention to the all-pervasive assumption that the aged have to have things done *for* them by other people."

Everyone at the media conference thought that television commercials were the worst offenders, both in neglecting older people or in presenting them in disrespectful ways—but one newsman suggested that television commercials insult everyone. Advertising was also blamed for the fact that old people are too ready to accept society's low esteem: "We never see ourselves as potential buyers of anything except cookies, laxatives, and false teeth."

Years ago, when my thoughts about age were more likely to be related to my children's birthday parties, I met a producer for NBC news and told him how offensive I found the incessant commercials for dentures and laxatives on the dinner-hour news. That timing, he informed me, was no accident. The eleven o'clock news was presumed to be watched by the young, the seven o'clock by the old. Money is money and the devil with sensibilities; times haven't changed on the early evening news.

Obviously, the products are selling or the commercials would be off the air. But not everyone who watches those programs is old, and older people do buy other products. As *Media Decisions* pointed out in its October 1977 issue, the 55-plus age group is a 200-*billion*-dollar market. It wouldn't cost the networks a cent to downplay the stereotype of older people that those ads reinforce, day after day, year after year.

One suggestion made at the media conference was to boycott offending advertisers. Advertising and broadcast representatives thought that pressure tactics would work.

What's in a Name?

Says Dr. Butler, "No racial or ethnic group would accept the epithets that are applied to old people."

While Butler was referring to such obviously derogatory terms as old geezer, old crock, old bag, or turkey (popular with your lovable family-doctor-to-be, the intern) I think the issue is more serious when it comes to "friendly" names. I am sure the young staff worker of a community center didn't mean to sound patronizing when he wrote me about "our wonderful seniors."

At the media conference, terms used to refer to older people were considered important and discussed in most of the workshops. Although no one designation was completely agreed upon, a number were thoroughly disliked. Euphemisms like "golden age" and "sunset years" led the list, with "senior citizen" the next most unpopular. (Senior citizen centers used to be called golden age clubs; more and more they are now, simply, senior centers. In another clue to the hoped-for demise of "senior citizen," the *New York Times* style book, reflecting the opinion of many readers, advises writers to avoid the words whenever possible. The National Council on the Aging, in a brochure directed to writers and producers, asks, "What would have happened to the sales of a book called *The Senior Citizen and the Sea*?")

The terms that were most preferred at the media conference were "older people" and "old." "Over 60" was dismissed because it implied a sharp dividing line between the young and the old. It also implies that at a certain specified time of life a person stops being himself and suddenly turns into an old person.

For myself, I have felt most comfortable with "older people" because that term does not connote any particular age. You can accept the designation or not and interpret it as you like. The title of this book does imply that I have a specific age in mind, but that, of course, is a semiserious play on the national speed limit cum commentary on how this country looks at older people.

Drawing by G. Kerlin; © 1978, The New Yorker Magazine, Inc.

CHAPTER 3

Down with Ageism, Up with the Activists: Maggie Kuhn and the Gray Panthers

In August of 1970, when Margaret Kuhn's employers forced her to give up her job because she had reached the mandatory retirement age of 65, they could hardly have foreseen what they were unleashing. Yet perhaps they should have—for forty-three years she had worked in church-related organizations in the field of social change.

Within a month, Maggie and five friends, all of whom were retiring from national religious and social work organizations, began meeting to discuss what they were going to do with the rest of their lives. They looked at the common problems that face most retired people: a loss of income, loss of contact with associates, and loss of one of the most important identity roles of our society, one's job. But in addition to difficulties, they also discovered a new kind of freedom, the freedom to support openly those things they believed in, such as their opposition to the Vietnam War, as they were not able to do within the bureaucracies they worked for.

Throughout the summer the group met, grew, and began to reach out to college students to support them in their opposition to the war and the draft. Out of these meetings came an organization called the Consultation of Older and Younger Adults for Social Change. With a name like that, the organization might never have gotten out of Philadelphia, where it began and where the national office of the Gray Panthers is today. A New York television producer dubbed Maggie and her fellow activists with the name Gray Panthers; later the newspapers took it up and it stuck.

Just a few months after Maggie and her friends started meeting, they took their first concerted action; in a small way it was a forerunner in

Gray Panther Maggie Kuhn, in a typical pose—raised fist and broad smile—gives her rallying cry, "Off your asses!," to the national convention of the Gray Panthers. *Photo credit: Julie Jensen*

Isadore Levitt, a Boston Gray Panther, reading a poem he wrote in honor of Maggie Kuhn at the 1977 Panther convention. Studs Terkel is at the left. *Photo credit: Julie Jensen*

both style and content of the direction the Gray Panthers would eventually take. In September of 1970, task forces began meeting in preparation for the 1971 White House Conference on Aging. Maggie's group was both skeptical about the conference and determined to influence the policies it was supposed to formulate. Several members served on preparatory task force groups and others got themselves press credentials; at the conference, they protested the managed news that was given the press.

Others became active in the leadership of a national conference of black and Puerto Rican older adults—during the Conference on Aging, seventy delegates invaded the White House grounds to demand a shift in priorities from war to human services.

As the group grew, the emphasis turned inevitably to the needs and ideas of its own constituency. In 1973, Ralph Nader's Retired Professional Action Group joined forces with the Gray Panthers. Nader-type action is a natural for the Panthers. During a five-day meeting of the American Medical Association in Chicago, when, in spite of their income from Medicare, the doctors hadn't scheduled a single discussion related to health care for older people, the Gray Panthers—as the headlines put it—"gave the needle to the AMA." With cameramen and reporters in attendance, a group of Gray Panthers conducted some lively street theater outside the Palmer House. Paying a house call on the sick AMA, they carried its "body" to a waiting ambulance for resuscitation. When oxygen and mouth-to-mouth breathing failed to re-

Expect a Lot

"When you get to be my age and you have one of those days when you just don't feel quite up to par, very often you find that people don't take your aches and pains all that seriously. Your doctor will offer you some standard advice, prescribe some pill, and may even ask you, as your family and friends have done many times: 'What do you expect at your age?'

"Well, let me tell you something; I expect a lot.

"I expect a lot because I believe that each and every one of us, regardless of how old we are, not only can, but should, expect a lot. Lower your expectations, or give them up entirely, and you'll end up getting exactly what you expected: little or nothing.

"Think of the message you are communicating when you ask them, 'What do you expect at your age?' You're telling people what they can expect and what they can't expect. You're telling them they can expect to suffer increasingly from the so-called infirmities of age. And you're telling them they can't expect anyone else to take those infirmities very seriously.

"There's only one thing wrong with all that, and it's this: Age has no infirmities. Only human beings do."

From "Senior Report with Maggie Kuhn," a twice-a-week television spot. Stations interested in carrying "Senior Report" should write or call:

Alcare Communications, Inc.
P.O. Box 361
Wayne, PA 19087
215-687-5767

vive the AMA, they tried deep chest massage, and discovered a wad of money around the heart, which restricted its action. When the attending Gray Panthers removed the money, the patient quickly revived.

The Panthers' demands to the AMA House of Delegates included: geriatric courses in medical schools, consumer representation on AMA committees, and basic changes in the "sickness care" system.

One of the issues the Nader group had been working on was an investigation of the hearing-aid industry. Their report, *Paying Through the Ear,* which showed that many companies were defrauding citizens with hearing problems, was taken over by the Panthers, who continue to monitor the industry and work for legislation to protect consumers. *A Citizens' Guide for Nursing Home Reform,* published by the Gray Panthers, also grew out of the Nader group's research. Again, the Panthers are continuing to investigate nursing homes, organizing residents, and working for the training of nurses' aides in proper care.

As clients of the National Senior Citizens Law Center, the Gray Panthers have taken the battle against ageism to the courts on a number of fronts. In *Gray Panthers* v. *Califano,* the Panthers are suing to require Medicare to hold hearings for all disputes, regardless of the money involved. Other suits involve age discrimination in employment, and the rights of participants in a pension fund to know the probabilities of their not receiving benefits, and to sue the fund for fraud for not revealing that information.

It would be reverse stereotyping to call Maggie Kuhn and the Gray Panthers typical of the new older generation. Still, their almost irrepressible growth from a loose-knit group of like-minded people to a nationwide intergenerational network (and now a strong national organization) is the best indication that older people like the Panthers' style. They are activists with a sense of humor and total irreverence for the sacred cows of the aging establishment, from the American Gerontological Society to senior citizen centers, which Maggie Kuhn calls "playpens for the old."

With their raised-fist salute, T-shirts emblazoned with a sweetly smiling pussycatlike panther, and their leader's ringing cry of "Off your asses!" the Panthers may put to rest forever the stereotype of what a proper old-age advocacy group should be.

Indeed, their success in this area has given the Panthers some image problems of their own, since they feel strongly that they "are not just another interest group for the elderly," but "are dedicated to improving the quality of life for all people." The group takes seriously its full name—Gray Panthers, Age and Youth in Action—and at its May 1978 meeting, the national steering committee adopted this statement:

Due to increasingly frequent and grossly inaccurate media portrayals of the Gray Panthers as either another "interest group for the elderly," or the increasingly frequent use of the term "Gray Panther" as a generic term to represent "senior power activists," the Gray Panther National Steering Committee requests that local Gray Panther networks and task forces aggressively and intentionally reassert that:

1. We are NOT a vested interest group for the elderly.
2. We are NOT out to win points for older people at the expense of other groups.
3. We ARE a movement composed of ALL ages dedicated to changing people's ideas about aging.
4. We ARE a movement dedicated to improving the quality of life for ALL people.

The Gray Panthers is organized through a national office, task forces, and local networks. The address of the national office is:

Gray Panthers
3700 Chestnut Street
Philadelphia, PA 19104

Gray Panther Task Forces

The national Gray Panthers maintain a number of active task forces, each of which concentrates on a particular aspect created by ageism in our society. For information on how to work in the area that interests you, write to the contact person at the address given, or work through your local Gray Panther network (see below).

Media Watch Project

The Media Watch was formed in 1974 "in response to complaints relative to the negative and often offensive images of older people in the media." The committee maintains that "the image of old people now being portrayed is wholly unrealistic . . . Older characterizations, when they do appear, are presented in distorted and stereotypic ways . . . As older people, we are functioning adults . . . and we want to be shown that way. We want to be shown as human beings taking an active part in society, interacting with all ages." (For more on the Media Watch, see chapter 2.)

To become involved or report an incident, write:

Lydia Bragger
Gray Panther Media Watch
1841 Broadway, Room 300
New York, NY 10023

Task Force on a New Economic System

A twenty-four-page pamphlet entitled "Economic Rights—Economic Democracy: A Working Paper for Study by the Gray Panther Movement," has just been published by this task force. The paper by the "radical Gray Panther economists," according to the organization's newspaper, *Network,* is expected to become one of the most widely discussed documents published by the Gray Panthers. Single copies are available for $1. A section-by-section study guide with a bibliography is also available— $2 for the pamphlet and study guide. Copies may be obtained from the national office.

For information about the Task Force on a New Economic System, write:

G. Shubert Frye
Hortonville, NY 12745

Task Force on Housing

These "rubble-rousers" have been involved in interracial housing fights in Washington for the past six years. The task force will expand its activities to explore new kinds of public housing, including congregate housing and communal living ("anything but senior high-rises"). It has also been given the responsibility of working more closely with disabled groups and others looking for alternative lifestyles, including intergenerational housing.

For information, write:
Joe Davis, Chairperson
Task Force on Housing
4534 47th Street, N.W.
Washington, DC 20016

Task Force on Health

A plan for radical surgery on the health care system calls for "amputation of the fee-for-service system, the drug mills, and private health insurance—i.e., a national health service."

For information, write:
Frances Klafter
1734 P Street, N.W.
Washington, DC 20036
or
Glen Gersmehl
525 E. 5th Street
New York, NY 10009

Task Force on Youth

This task force is determined "to get the second half of the Gray Panthers off the ground" so that the organization can truly call itself Age and Youth in Action. Issues to be addressed include compulsory education, alternative living arrangements, voting rights, and sexuality.

For information, write:
Sarah Luria
c/o The Gray Panthers
3700 Chestnut Street
Philadelphia, PA 19104

Task Force on the Older Poor

This task force will concentrate on retirement and pension plans, property taxes, and welfare programs. The Gray Panthers have entered a class action suit with the National Senior Citizens Law Center over civil rights in conservatorship and guardianship proceedings.

For information, write:
Barbe Creagh
c/o The Gray Panthers
3700 Chestnut Street
Philadelphia, PA 19104

Task Force on Employment

An end to mandatory retirement is only a first step toward the Gray Panthers' goal on employment; the ultimate aim is full employment. Meanwhile, the task force is working toward reform of CETA and other government job programs (see chapter 7).

For information, write:
Ed Marcus
P.O. Box 1802
Hollywood, FL 33022

Task Force on Older Women

In conjunction with the National Organization for Women's Task Force on Older Women, this group will work, first, to mobilize support for the Equal Rights Amendment and then to move key legislative items, such as the Displaced Homemakers Bill, designed specifically to alleviate the problems of older women.

For information, write:
Rita Wreck
c/o The Gray Panthers
3700 Chestnut Street
Philadelphia, PA 19104

Task Force on Transportation

Reports *Network*, "Here is an issue that links people in urban, suburban, and rural communities: fragmented and inadequate mass transportation services. Enough is enough, and this task force is determined to take down the barriers and do something about the blight of freeways and land use planning."

For information, write:
Sylvia Wexler
150 W. 96th Street
New York, NY 10025
or
Artie Deutsch
601 Market Street
San Diego, CA 92101

Task Force on Minority Outreach

After making some "honest observations" about the under-representation of "oppressed minorities" at the 1977 Gray Panthers convention, this task force is preparing to send local Gray Panthers networks guidelines and action strategies for dealing in discrimination struggles at the grassroots level.

For information, write:
Irving Wiesenfeld
609 Columbus Avenue, #6Q
New York, NY 10025

Networks

Gray Panther Networks are continually organizing. If you don't find a Network in your area on this list, write to the national office.

The Gray Panthers
3700 Chestnut Street
Philadelphia, PA 19104

Alabama
Alabama Gray Panthers
Cindy McCartney
605 Merit Springs Road
Gadsden, AL 35901

Arizona
Tucson Gray Panthers
Les Farkas
448 W. Matterhorn
Tucson, AZ 85704

California
Gray Panthers of the East Bay, Inc.
2131 University Avenue, Room 303
Berkeley, CA 94704

Central Contra Costa County Panthers
Annelle Rouse
1841 Laguna Street, #324
Concord, CA 94520

Santa Clara County Gray Panthers
Richard Gregory
10827 Minette Drive
Cupertino, CA 95104

Cupertino Court Gray Panthers
V. Lyle Field
19140 Stevens Creek Boulevard
Cupertino, CA 95014

West Contra Costa County Gray Panthers
Fancheon Christner
2023 Key Boulevard
El Cerrito, CA 94530

Santa Cruz County Gray Panthers
Sue Wanenmacher
435 Creekside Way
Felton, CA 95018

Fresno Gray Panthers
June Silkwood
3345 Mayfair Drive N.
Fresno, CA 93703

Rio Hondo Gray Panthers
Morris Better
2401 S. Hacienda Boulevard, #K-141
Hacienda Heights, CA 91745

Laguna Hills Gray Panthers
Minna Liebman
739A Avenida Majorca
Laguna Hills, CA 92653

Long Beach Gray Panthers
Cora Cocks
2450 Pine Avenue
Long Beach, CA 90806

Andrus Gray Panthers
Stephanie Dollinger
Andrus Gerontology Center
University of Southern California
Los Angeles, CA 90007

Beverly-Fairfax Gray Panthers
Slyana Singer Dreyfus
122 N. Flores
Los Angeles, CA 90048

Central Los Angeles Gray Panthers
Rose N. Marshall
612 N. Beachwood
Los Angeles, CA 90004

West Los Angeles Gray Panthers
Lillian Schuman
10709 Ashton Avenue
Los Angeles, CA 90024

Gray Panthers of Marin
Dorothy Belcher
74 Alta Vista Avenue
Mill Valley, CA 94941

Mid-Valley Network of San Fernando Valley
Ilene Savitt
12762 Willard Street
North Hollywood, CA 91605

San Fernando Valley Gray Panthers
Dorace Deigh
3650 Alta Mesa Drive
North Hollywood, CA 91604

Oakland/Emeryville Gray Panthers
Rose Della Monica
c/o A Central Place
1221 Broadway, Room 390
Oakland, CA 94612

Orange County Gray Panthers
Greg Bishop
146 N. Grand Street
Orange, CA 92666

San Mateo County Gray Panthers
Delia Vicerra
293 Modoc Place
Pacifica, CA 94044

Sacramento Gray Panthers
Orinne Sherman
5166 Connecticut Avenue
Sacramento, CA 95821

Santa Monica/Venice Gray Panthers
Hanna Jaffee
1325 Centinela Avenue
Santa Monica, CA 90404

San Diego Gray Panthers
Artie Deutsch
601 Market Street
San Diego, CA 92101

San Francisco Gray Panthers
Sister Mary Jennie Sandford
214 Haight Street
San Francisco, CA 94102

San Jose Gray Panthers
Alvin Bach
290 Village Court
San Jose, CA 95110

South Bay Gray Panthers
Dr. Herbert Lee Swanson
El Camino College
16007 Crenshaw Boulevard
Torrance, CA 90506

Greater Los Angeles Gray Panthers
Abe Boxerman
6044 Greenbush
Van Nuys, CA 91401

Colorado
Boulder Gray Panthers
Betty Lane
2227 Canyon Boulevard, Apt. 204
Boulder, CO 80302

Denver Gray Panthers
Anne Fenerty
1400 Lafayette Street
Denver, CO 80218

Connecticut
Greater Hartford Gray Panthers
Joel Schwartz
350 Farmington Avenue
Hartford, CT 06105

Greater New Haven Gray Panthers
Jim Shannon, Sage Advocate
53 Wall Street
New Haven, CT 06510

Fairfield County Gray Panthers
First United Methodist Church
Cross Road
Stamford, CT 06905

District of Columbia
Gray Panthers of Metropolitan Washington, DC
Calvary Baptist Church
711 8th Street, N.W.
Washington, DC 20001

Florida
Broward County Gray Panthers
Edward E. Marcus
1150 Hayes Street
Hollywood, FL 33022

Miami Gray Panthers
Elena Herrschaft
First Unitarian Church
7701 S.W. 76th Avenue
Miami, FL 33143

Sarasota Gray Panthers
Phyllis R. Kaplan
Box 3492
Sarasota, FL 33578

Georgia
Gray Panthers of Athens
Dr. Thomas M. Goolsby, Jr.
P.O. Box 4294 Campus Station
Athens, GA 30602

Atlanta Gray Panthers
Bob Titus
Catholic Social Services, Inc.
756 W. Peachtree Street, N.W.
Atlanta, GA 30308

Augusta Gray Panthers
Sister Cathan Miles
1325 Greene Street
Augusta, GA 38902

Illinois
Chicago Gray Panthers
Henrietta Moore and Ruth Lind
343 S. Dearborn Street, Room 718
Chicago, IL 60604

Indiana
Evansville Gray Panthers
Susan Hagedorn
Community Action Program
906 Main Street
Evansville, IN 47771

Iowa
Black Hawk Gray Panthers
Irma Gossman
204 Linden Avenue
Waterloo, IA 50703

Kentucky
Lexington Gray Panthers
Leslie Mayette
1696 Hill Rise Drive, Apt. 8
Lexington, KY 40505

Louisville Gray Panthers
Joan Johnson
4109 Pecunnie Way
Louisville, KY 40218

Maine
Maine Gray Panther Network
Mary Mohler
The Salvation Army
297 Cumberland Avenue
Portland, ME 04111

Maryland
Howard County Gray Panthers
Florence Rowley
6043-2 Majors Lane
Columbia, MD 21045

Maryland Network No. 1
Margaret Stanton
United Church Center
114 W. Montgomery Avenue
Rockville, MD 20858

Maryland Advocates for the Aging
Bernard L. Talley
6 Southfield Place
Baltimore, MD 21212

Massachusetts
Gray Panthers of Greater Boston
Elsie Reethof
1 Chauncy Street, No. 3
Cambridge, MA 02138

Springfield Gray Panthers
Edward Johnston
6 Sorrento Street
Springfield, MA 01108

Michigan
Michigan Gray Panthers
Eric Glatz
18467 Pine West
Wyandotte, MI 48192

Minnesota
Twin Cities Gray Panthers
Vonnie Lowman and Ronelda Gutknecht
University of Minnesota
Minneapolis, MN 55455

Mississippi
Jackson Gray Panthers
Eddie Sandifer
2541 Coronet Place
Jackson, MS 39204

Missouri
Kansas City Gray Panthers
Cecilia Raske
Community Services Department
City Hall
Kansas City, MO 64106

Montana
Gray Panthers of Montana
Patrick M. McLaughlin
Box 1314
Billings, MT 59103

Nebraska
Lincoln Gray Panthers
Esther Hamon
1426 S. 20th Street
Lincoln, NE 68508

Omaha Gray Panthers
Doris Mendes
700 N. 20th Street
Omaha, NE 68102

Nevada
Gray Panthers of Nevada
Eugene G. Greene
3667 El Camino Road
Las Vegas, NV 89103

New Hampshire
New Hampshire Gray Panthers
Elna Perkins
5 Fourth Avenue
Rochester, NH 03806

New Jersey
Gray Panthers of Bergen Co.
Louise Fontaine
70 State Street
Teaneck, NJ 07666

Burlington Gray Panthers
Howard Kreckman
Beech Nut Lane
Martins Beach, NJ 08016

New Brunswick Gray Panthers
Linda Eckart
P.O. Box 101
Rutgers Mental Health Clinic
Piscataway, NJ 08854

South Jersey Gray Panthers
Doris Campbell
903 Point Street
Camden, NJ 08102

Don't Agonize — Organize

"Real personhood throughout our entire life spans is fundamentally as revolutionary an idea as equality of the sexes, with implications that will affect all our institutions. For example, the contradiction of setting up roadblocks to working as we grow older, then complaining about the cost of providing for an ever-increasing non-working population, will seem ridiculous . . .

"But when it comes to ageism, we're hardly out of the rocking chair. Of course we elders are going to have to take the lead. Nobody liberates anybody else. We have to do that for ourselves. When we finally recognize that the main problem of the aged lies not with ourselves but in the nature of a society that allocates persons in the prime of life to the junk heap, and when we become angry enough to get together and perhaps throw a picket line around the junk heap and say, 'I will not be scrapped—I have a third of my life to go' . . . *Then,* we will be in good enough shape to change things around so you who are forty or even (God forbid) thirty and feeling old, will have a better place to age in . . .

"There is nothing that changes the image of a powerless group faster than rattling the cages. 'Don't agonize—organize' is our slogan."

From a speech by Tish Sommers, "free-lance agitator" and coordinator of the NOW Older Women's Rights Committee.

New York

Gray Panthers of SUNY/Buffalo
Jack Kramer
115 Little Robin Road
West Amherst, NY 14228

New York Gray Panthers
Fannie Krasnon and Stella Murphy
15 W. 65th Street, Room 311
New York, NY 10023

Long Island City Gray Panthers
Peggy Wieri
39-20 45th Street
Long Island City, NY 11104

Central Queens Gray Panthers
Evelyn Neleson
73-72 194th Street
Flushing, NY 11366

Suffolk County Gray Panthers
Catherine Brava
149 Dougherty Avenue
Holbrook, NY 11741

Gray Panthers of Rockland County
Moses Zuckerman
14 B Street
Pomona, NY 10970

Ohio

Akron Gray Panthers
John Looney
c/o Humanity House
475 W. Market Street
Akron, OH 44306

Cincinnati Gray Panthers
Clare Brauer
501 Rentz Place
Cincinnati, OH 45238

Miami Valley Gray Panther Network
Hilda E. Will
5081 Silver Dome Road
Dayton, OH 45414

Advocates for the Aged
Joy Teckenbrock
120 E. Foraker Avenue
Dayton, OH 45409

Dayton Gray Panthers
Linda Favorite
105 S. Wilkinson
Dayton, OH 45402

Citizens on the Move at YMCA
Deana Pippin
YMCA
117 W. Monument Avenue
Dayton, OH 45402

Columbus Wedgewood Gray Panthers
Franklinton Gray Panthers
Linda Spengler
3633 Wilbur Avenue
Grove City, OH 43123

Warren Gray Panthers
Juanita B. Trice
400 Second Street
Warren, OH 44483

Greene County Gray Panthers
Andre Bognar
Greenwood Manor
711 Dayton-Xenia Road
Xenia, OH 45385

Oregon

Lake Oswego Gray Panthers
Ann Schukart
P.O. Box 224
Lake Oswego, OR 97034

Newport Gray Panthers
Jo Norgorden
423B S.W. Elizabeth
Newport, OR 97365

Portland Gray Panthers
Ruth Haefner
4242 N.E. Failing
Portland, OR 97213

Pennsylvania

Pennsylvania Capital Gray Panthers
William T. Coombs
2 Stone Spring Lane
Camp Hill, PA 17011

Philadelphia Gray Panthers
George Ammon
3700 Chestnut Street
Philadelphia, PA 19104

Western Pennsylvania Gray Panthers
Ethel Hazo
127 S. Fairmount
Pittsburgh, PA 15206

Rhode Island

Rhode Island Gray Panthers
Michael M. Boday
Centennial Towers, Apt. 301
35 Goff Avenue
Pawtucket, RI 02860

Tennessee

Knoxville Gray Panthers
Steve W. Roberts
P.O. Box 16367
Knoxville, TN 37916

Memphis Delta Gray Panthers
Isabel G. Reilly
P.O. Box 4774
Memphis, TN 38104

Texas

Austin Gray Panthers
Arthelia Cook Smith
3415 West Avenue
Austin, TX 78705

Gray Panthers of Greater Houston
  Esther Faerber
  3902 Villanova
  Houston, TX 77005

Bexar County Gray Panthers
  Lt. Col. Jos. DiGiacomo
  1036 W. Russell Place
  San Antonio, TX 78212

Vermont
Vermont Gray Panthers
  Faire Edwards
  55 S. Main Street
  Waterbury, VT 05676

Washington
Kittitas Valley Gray Panthers
  Isabel Callison
  Box 617
  Kittitas, WA 98934

Thurston County Gray Panthers
  Milton D. Lowenstein
  P.O. Box 2355
  Olympia, WA 98507

Seattle Gray Panthers
  Jack Slee
  Good Shepherd Center
  4649 Sunnyside N.
  Seattle, WA 98103

Spokane Gray Panthers
  Jim Warner
  3534 W. Wellesler
  Spokane, WA 99205

Olympia Gray Panthers
  Rebecca Johnson
  411 West Lee, #K2
  Tumwater, WA 98502

West Virginia
Charleston Gray Panthers
  Della Mickel
  1546 Kanawha Boulevard
  E. Charleston, WV 25311

Wisconsin
Madison Gray Panthers
  Mildred Kreager
  517 N. Franklin Drive
  Madison, WI 53705

Part II

Staying Active

CHAPTER 4

Education — New Programs for Older People

When he was 80, the Roman Statesman Cato the Elder began to study Greek. To a friend who asked why he was starting out on such a large task at such an advanced age, Cato replied that it was the youngest age he had left.

More than two thousand years later, 70-year-old Mrs. Zelda Stanke of Belleville, Wisconsin, spent a year in the Live-In-and-Learn program at the University of Wisconsin's Whitewater campus. She enjoyed it so much she convinced her 93-year-old mother, Mrs. Mollie Fritz, to join her in the on-campus living and learning experiment.

While they are hardly typical, these two unusual college roommates point up one of the most remarkable phenomena in education in recent years. By the hundreds of thousands, maybe millions, older people are going back to the classroom—every kind of classroom. They are turning the concept of lifelong learning, a few years ago just tentatively espoused by educational theorists, into a reality. And they aren't going back on sufferance, either, because as the numbers of students of traditional age drops, many educational institutions are looking for the non-traditional students, both out of a conviction that lifelong learning is the new wave, and as a way of staying in business.

What is the older student studying? Everything. One surprising statistic comes from Ann Marcus, Dean of New York University's School of Continuing Education, which has 32,000 students. Ten years ago, Dr. Marcus said, adult education stressed the liberal arts. Today the programs are more specifically career-oriented. In a survey of 2500 students in the Management Institute, which offers courses in public relations, communications, marketing and advertising, personnel, and similar subjects, Dr. Marcus found that a surprising 16 percent of the students in this career-training program were over 62.

In their book, *You Are Never Too Old to Learn,* Wilbur Cross and Carol Florio report on a survey taken by the Academy for Educational Development. Program directors at several hundred colleges and universities with large numbers of older students were asked what were the most popular subjects with these students. "The answers," wrote the authors, "may be surprising to those people who persist in believing that as we grow more experienced with life, we tend to lose interest in it." The nine most popular subjects were history, psychology, health, foreign languages, literature, painting, creative writing, religion, and needlework. Philosophy, preretirement planning, and physical fitness were tied for tenth place. "All in all, a pretty healthy mix."

According to the *New York Times,* the number of colleges and universities offering courses to retirement-aged people has multiplied twenty-five times in the 1970s. Although most of these are two-year community colleges or junior colleges, four-year institutions have also started programs for older people. And even if they haven't, a great many colleges and universities allow older students both to audit and take courses for credit. In addition, of course, there are adult education programs or continuing education programs, open to anyone. Older people can often take these courses without charge. A variety of nonacademic organizations also offer courses for older people, notably the Institute of Lifetime Learning (see below) sponsored by the American Association for Retired Persons and the National Retired Teachers Association. Many of these are co-sponsored by local colleges and universities. The most innovative program of all is Elderhostel, also described in this chapter.

Because it would be impossible and not useful to list every institution that offers courses for older people or admits them to regular classes, the college programs described in this chapter are some of the more unusual ones designed specifically for the older age group. Most of these same schools also admit older people to many of their regular classes.

The Institute of Lifetime Learning has recently completed a survey of tuition policies of colleges and universities throughout the country and has compiled a list of those that provide free or reduced tuition for older people. To find out the names of these institutions in your state, write:

Tuition Study
Institute of Lifetime Learning
1909 K Street, N.W.
Washington, DC 20049

In spite of the boom in traditional and nontraditional classroom programs for older people, with the social as well as intellectual stimulation of being in an educational environment, there are, obviously, some people who cannot get to them. If you live in a rural area or are homebound, you can still pursue an education. For a list of universities that offer independent study programs through their extension departments, write:

National University Extension Association
Suite 360
1 DuPont Circle, N.W.
Washington, DC 20036

For a free directory of accredited schools that offer home-study courses, write:

National Home Study Council
1601 18th Street, N.W.
Washington, DC 20009

Elderhostel

In the summer of 1975, five New Hampshire colleges, in a small pilot project, opened their campuses to "hostelers" of retirement age. The first week, five people enrolled; by the end of the summer, only 220 had taken part in the program, filling a disappointing 65 percent of the available spaces.

One year later, as a result of the publicity the experiment received, twenty-one New England colleges had Elderhostel programs. More than 2000 people were enrolled and another thousand had to be turned away. From that moment, there was no holding the Elderhostel movement—by 1978, there were hostel programs at colleges in twenty states, with an enrollment of more than 7000 people.

What is Elderhostel? For one 79-year-old woman, "it is the only positive thing that has happened to me as a *result* of being old."

In more concrete terms, it is a network of colleges and universities that offer special low-cost, one-week residential programs for older people during the summer months. Participants use the network for an educational hosteling experience, moving from campus to campus, taking the courses that appeal to them, and exploring the interesting cultural and environmental resources of the local area. Each week-long program is limited to thirty or forty members to provide for an informal atmosphere in which making friends is easy.

The range of courses offered and the variety of college sites is enormous. From the Appalachian Mountains of North Carolina to the Iowa plains to the lakes of New England, colleges offer studies on virtually every aspect of the human experience—except one. The Elderhostel institutions are given only two guidelines. The first is that the courses have an intellectual content and quality equal to the average offerings of the college. The second is that no college may offer Elderhostelers any course designed for the elderly. "Elderhostel is not interested in teaching people to be old," says Martin Knowlton, one of the two men who thought up the whole idea.

Knowlton and David Bianco, both of the University of New Hampshire, conceived of Elderhostel "in a surge of idealism and concern, with the conviction that one of the major problems of aging lies with the self-image of uselessness and futility that United States society foists on its older members."

After a couple of summers of experience with Elderhostel, Knowlton admitted that "our naiveté in thinking that a week of classes on a college campus could reverse this self-image astounds us. But the fact that the idea really works overwhelms us."

Hostels have for centuries been places of temporary shelter and repose for people on the move. "Elderhostel," says Knowlton, "is for older citizens on the move—not necessarily in terms of physical movement and travel, but in the sense of reaching out to new experience."

In any one-week period on campus, Elderhostelers can take up to three courses, taught by regular faculty members. There are no grades, no exams, no required homework, although students may ask the faculty for assignments. No previous formal training is necessary and participants have ranged from those with a grammar-school education to Ph.D.s. In a study made of the 1976 group, about 70 percent had some college education. Nineteen percent were former professionals; the same number were teachers; 51 percent were white-collar workers; 9 percent listed themselves as housewives; and 2 percent as blue-collar workers.

Although the bottom cut-off age was 60, very few of the Elderhostelers that year were under 65. The median age was 68 and the average age was 70. Three out of four were women and very few of the men were single.

In addition to the courses, the campus weeks include social events, museum tours, summer theaters, nature walks, and song fests with the students. The events, like the courses, vary from campus to campus.

Each college sets aside one dormitory for the Elderhostelers. Where possible, it is chosen for easy access and proximity to classrooms and dining halls. Since it isn't always possible and some campuses are on hilly sites, the hostelers often find themselves walking more than usual, with the side effect that many people have reported an improvement in their feelings of health after a hostel week. (However, the regional offices, which coordinate the registration, do take care to direct people with physical handicaps to campuses that require less walking and can offer elevators or ramps.)

At all campuses, intellectual and spiritual considerations are given higher priority than creature comforts. Few college dormitories are in any way luxurious. The rooms are simple, bathrooms are usually communal, and no New England college is air conditioned. Hostelers eat in the cafeteria with other summer students.

Since Elderhostels are nonprofit, geared to people on fixed incomes, the colleges charge less than their normal rates for tuition, room, and board. The range is about $60 to $100 a week. Nevertheless, there is a major concern that the program be accessible to anyone who wants to enroll, and the regional offices as well as the individual colleges conduct year-round searches for extra funds for hostelships. People who could not otherwise attend are encouraged to ask for financial assistance. Recipients are not asked embarrassing questions or required to prove their need; they simply check the appropriate place on the registration form.

Courses cover the entire spectrum of the liberal arts curriculum. They range from genetic engineering to developing outdoor skills, from the changing American family to tropical plant families, from discovering percussion music to new currents in American law and government. Colleges located in historic or environmentally unusual areas offer courses that have particular significance to their locations. Thus, in North Carolina the ten Elderhostel colleges have many courses about the Appalachian region.

If Elderhostel is, as they say in the education business, a learning experience, the hostelers are not the only learners. Knowlton, director of the New England program, gleefully recalls a telephone call he received from a 23-year-old dormitory manager. It seemed a 95-year-old man wanted to share a room with his 70-year-old woman friend; what should she do? "Well," replied Knowlton dryly, "if you want to act *in loco parentis* to a 95-year-old man, go right ahead."

Faculty members, in some cases where the program is new, have been reluctant to participate. When Amherst College announced its first Elderhostel, which would run for four weeks, only four of the needed twelve professors signed up and the rest had to be recruited from other colleges. Naturally enough, Amherst decided it could manage only a two-week hostel program the second year. But this time so many of its own faculty members wanted to be included that the schedule was expanded to eight weeks.

Not all teachers have their doubts, even in the beginning. One such man, Harley Henry, Professor of English at Macalaster College in Minnesota, saw this as a golden opportunity to build a course around his own obsession with baseball. Harley's 1978 Elderhostel course was "Diamonds in the Rough: The Significance of Our National Pastime." Henry is not only a fan but a serious student of the history of baseball and the literary works inspired by it. Naturally, his course included a field trip to a Minnesota Twins game.

Although it is impossible to give a true picture of the variety of offerings all over the country, a list of the courses offered in 1978 in North Carolina alone may give some idea of what an Elderhosteler can find in a summer:

Appalachian State University
   Television Production
   An Introduction to the Works of William Faulkner
   The Search for Extraterrestrial Life
   History of the Appalachian Region
   Southern Appalachian Flora
   Southern Appalachian Religious Philosophy and Beliefs

University of North Carolina at Wilmington
   The Marine Environment: Earth's Last Frontier
   Giants in American Religion
   Nautical Literature
   The South and the Nation
   Music in the Imagination of Man
   A History of Colonial North Carolina

University of North Carolina at Asheville
   The Life and Literature of Thomas Wolfe
   Plants of the Blue Ridge Mountains
   Great Eastern Religions

University of North Carolina at Chapel Hill
   Exploring Space: The Strange and New
   Books and Ideas
   Chinese History in Art
   Ethics and Politics

University of North Carolina at Greensboro
   Developing Outdoor Skills
   Natural History
   Issues in Environmental Quality
   Seventeenth Century Devotional Poets
   Slavery, Moral Reform, and the Crisis of American Nationalism
   Education: The Way It Was, the Way It Is, the Way It Ought to Be
   The Ascent of Man
   The Emerging American Character
   American English Dialects

University of North Carolina at Charlotte
   Self-Expression Through Dance
   What It Means to Be Human
   Exploring the Cosmos

Duke University
   The New Deal: A Contemporary Assessment
   Shakespeare to Verdi: Othello and Otello
   Writing the Nostalgic Piece
   Cuba: From San Juan to Capitol Hill
   Being Human in the Contemporary World
   Nutrition: What We Do and Do Not Know
   Modern Poetry
   Medicine and Society
   Discovering the Past

Western Carolina University
Tracing Your Roots—Genealogy for
Beginners
Happiness: The Grand Pursuit
Appalachian Music and Dance
The American Indian: Fact and Fiction

Winston-Salem State University
Consumerism
Afro-American Music
Personalities of the Old Testament

Mars Hill College
Appalachian Music, Folklore, and Crafts
Appalachian Flora
Appalachian History and Contemporary
Social Issues

The regional catalogues give complete descriptions of the courses and the campus locations and facilities. Each region produces a catalogue sometime in the middle of March.

For further information, write the national office of Elderhostel of the region or regions of your choice.

Elderhostel, National Office
55 Chapel Street
Newton, MA 02160

Elderhostel, Florida Region
Eckerd College
St. Petersburg, FL 33733

Elderhostel, Iowa Region
C108 East Hall
University of Iowa
Iowa City, IA 52240

Elderhostel, Michigan Region
College of Health and Human Services
Western Michigan University
Kalamazoo, MI 49008

Elderhostel, Minnesota Region
206 Wesbrook Hall
77 Pleasant Street, S.W.
University of Minnesota
Minneapolis, MN 55435

Elderhostel, New England Region
New England Center for Continuing
Education
15 Garrison Avenue
Durham, NH 03824

Elderhostel, New York Region
New England Center for Continuing
Education
15 Garrison Avenue
Durham, NH 03824

Elderhostel, North Carolina Region
Continuing Education
UNC-CH Extension Division
209 Abernethy Hall 002-A
Chapel Hill, NC 27514

Elderhostel, Northwest Region
Center for Continuing Education
University of Montana
Missoula, MT 59812

Elderhostel, Ohio Region
Continuing Education
Baldwin Wallace College
Berea, OH 44017

Elderhostel, Pennsylvania Region
Educational Development Center
Shippensburg State College
Shippensburg, PA 17257

Elderhostel, Texas Region
  Abilene Christian University
  Box 7938
  Abilene Christian University Station
  Abilene, TX 79601

Elderhostel, West Virginia Region
  Psychology Department
  Fairmont State College
  Fairmont, WV 26554

Elderhostel, Wisconsin Region
  University of Wisconsin Extension
  Programs on Aging
  Marietta House
  3270 N. Marietta Avenue
  Milwaukee, WI 53201

Institute for Retired Professionals

Not surprisingly, the New School for Social Research in New York City, which was the country's first adult education university, was also the first to sponsor a special program for older retired people. The Institute of Retired Professionals, which opened in 1962, was for many years the only educational venture of its kind. Recently, a number of other colleges and universities, and at least one public-school adult education program, have started similar institutes on the New School model.

The IRP offers an opportunity for the many retired professionals in the New York City area to renew their education at the university level without the usual course procedures. Because of the life experience and interests of its members, it epitomizes a unique concept of adult education—its members are both teachers and students at the same time. All learn from each other. Thus, retired professionals and executives from teaching, law, medicine, government service, and business explore new interests and directions in their later years.

Membership in the IRP is open to people who have recently retired from a professional or executive career. Applicants must have suitable educational backgrounds and interests, and admission is determined after a review of the application by the membership committee. Today, the IRP has 650 members and a volunteer teaching faculty of one hundred. Approximately eighty courses or workshops are offered each year.

For the annual membership fee of $250, members may enroll in one of the New School's regular Adult Division courses each semester and participate in all phases of the IRP program. It is possible, for the person who wants to, to go back to school every day.

The IRP publishes a literary magazine, the *IRP Review,* and a newsletter. Members find social companionship both in the classes and on special trips and functions. In addition, the IRP Educational Extension Service provides speakers from its membership to senior citizen

A French play-reading group at the New School's Institute for Retired Professionals.

centers in the city. It also explores opportunities for involving IRP members as volunteers in educational institutions. And it continues to help other educational institutions to initiate programs for educated retired people. A 1976 workshop on this subject attracted representatives from almost sixty colleges and universities.

For information, write or call:
Dr. Hy Hirsch, Director
Institute for Retired Professionals
The New School
66 West 12th Street
New York, NY 10011
212-741-5682
HEIR (Higher Education in Retirement) is a new service of the New

School's IRP. This is an interinstitute newsletter designed to share information on retirement education programs. If you want information about starting such a program at your institution, the editors will send material and put you in touch with directors of similar programs. HEIR also welcomes clippings, brochures, or any other relevant material about other programs.

For information, write Michael Scott, Editor, HEIR, at the above address.

College at Sixty

Fordham University's alternative to retirement is The College at Sixty, designed for retired and pre-retired persons, 50 and over, whether or not

Members of the New School's Institute for Retired Professionals give a chamber music concert.

they have graduated from college. (The word *sixty* in the name refers to the location of the Fordham Lincoln Center campus, 113 West 60th Street in New York City.)

The college is primarily intended as a bridge to the regular academic program, although there is no requirement to matriculate. For those who do want to go on, admission to Fordham's Liberal Arts College is automatic after successful completion of four two-credit College at Sixty seminars. Students who want to study for the sheer pleasure of learning are more than welcome.

For the convenience of students who dislike commuting at night, classes are held in the morning and afternoon. They meet for two hours and run twelve weeks. During nonclass hours, The College at Sixty sponsors a lecture series and personal growth groups. Students may also use the library and the dining facilities of the faculty lounge.

The over-60 director of the college, Dr. Robert W. Adamson, a professor of philosophy, traces its genesis back to 1940 when his mother, at the age of 58, decided to study Russian history at Radcliffe. As a graduate of Smith College in 1904, she had no trouble being accepted, but once there she received little support for her action—classmates wondered what a woman of her age was doing in college—and after one semester she dropped out. Adamson was so moved by this incident that he resolved that at some point in his own career he would do something to help older people return effectively to academic life.

In the Fordham program, older adults can prepare themselves to reenter the youth-oriented regular liberal arts college in an intellectually stimulating, but supportive, community of peers. Adamson and his colleagues help the new students negotiate the often difficult passage from work to academic life. On the other hand, there is no relaxation of either academic standards or tuition prices—The College at Sixty doesn't believe in patronizing its older students. At optional weekly consciousness-raising groups, the problems of loneliness, role losses and changes, family stresses, and feelings of insecurity, as well as the cultural stereotypes of aging, are all up for discussion.

"Together we try to re-establish the students' self-esteem," says one of the professional leaders of these sessions. "Some of the people just entering the program are terribly blocked up. They act as if no one had given them permission to live. What I try to make them realize is that they don't need anyone's permission to live."

About 25 percent of the 150 students in the program—which continues to grow—are college graduates; some have never finished high school. They come from widely different economic, ethnic, racial, and religious backgrounds: a retired vice president of a New York City bank, a high-school dropout who had sent three sons to medical school, a daughter to law school, and another daughter to graduate school; a semiretired actor, as well as retired doctors, secretaries, firemen, homemakers, clergymen, teachers, businessmen, lawyers, and school custodians.

The College at Sixty recently received a three-year $100,000 grant to develop programs to train its students in such areas as oral history interviewing, pre-retirement counseling, and running for political office.

Tuition is $77 a credit, or $154 for a two-credit seminar. Grants-in-aid are available to those 60 and over who are unable to pay full tuition. Although there are no examinations or prerequisites for admission, other than a capacity to do college-level reading, writing, and discussion, an interview is required.

For further information, write or call:
The College at Sixty
Fordham University
Lincoln Center
113 West 60th Street
New York, NY 10023
212-956-3797

Fairhaven's Bridge

Fairhaven College, a semiautonomous campus of Western Washington State College, is perhaps the ultimate example of intergenerational learning. The 500-member student body ranges in age from 2 to 82. At the youngest end of the scale are the nursery-school children; at the oldest are thirty students in the Bridge Project, people over 55 who live in a campus apartment known as Bridgehouse. From the playground to Bridgehouse, the college walk symbolically passes two other groups of students—the "regular" collegians and the Older Returning Students, people from 25 to 60 years old who are matriculated in a degree program. (Bridgers may or may not study toward a degree.)

The Bridge Project grew out of two apparently unrelated but, as it turns out, complementary concerns—the lack of opportunities for retired adults and a falling enrollment, particularly of students who wanted to live in campus housing. (This turn toward older people to compensate for the decline in young students is by no means unique to Fairhaven. A cynic might see the academic community's interest in lifelong learning as an act of self-preservation. Nevertheless, if it serves all parties well, it is a healthy trend.)

For Fairhaven College and its students of all ages, the Bridge Project

Three generations of Fairhaven College students getting ready to backpack to Cape Alava on Washington's Olympic Peninsula to study the archaeological digs of an ancient Indian tribe. *Photo credit: Helen Warinsky*

is a unique and exciting venture. Still, it is not for everyone and not without its problems. In a survey of Bridge students, the most frequently given reasons for coming into the program were: classes amidst young people, campus activities, continuing education, and low-cost housing and food. Yet housing is perhaps the reason programs like this have not spread to other campuses. Young students who go away to college leave their parents' homes; older people either have to give up their homes or maintain them in addition to paying room and board at college. At the University of Wisconsin's Live-in-and-Learn program at the Whitewater campus, many learn but hardly anyone lives in.

In addition to the year-round program, the Bridge Project has a summer session that runs from approximately July 10 to August 18.

For information on the Bridge Project, write:

Doug Rich, Director
The Bridge Project
Fairhaven College
Bellingham, WA 98225

Older Adult Ed

The Academy for Retired Executives and Professionals, of Great Neck, Long Island, New York, is a self-run organization of one of the most innovative public-school adult education programs in the country. Started in 1972, REAP has almost one hundred members aged 55 to 86 who serve as teachers and students. The New School's IRP (see above) was the model, but its formalized structure did not work well in the suburban setting of Great Neck. Instead of classes, the REAP program is structured primarily around open seminars, planned well in advance, which everyone may attend. REAP rarely invites outside speakers.

Membership is not restricted by education and occupation but is open to anyone who can participate on the intellectual level of the group. Prospective members are urged to attend at least one session before they commit themselves to the program, which costs $35 a year.

REAP has become a model for communities that want to preserve the intellect and wisdom of older adults. A few other groups use the name, but there is no connection. REAP academies have been started in two other Long Island communities, Roslyn and Rockville Center.

For information, write:

Martin M. Stekert, Coordinator
Academy for Retired Executives and Professionals
Clover Drive Adult Center
105 Clover Drive
Great Neck, NY 11020

College Programs — State by State

California
University of California Extension Center

Center for Learning in Retirement
55 Laguna Street
San Francisco, CA 94102
Jeanne Brewer, Director

The Center for Learning in Retirement is a membership community of people who are approaching or who have already reached retirement. It is open to those who have an appetite for learning and an interest in intellectual and self-development activities. Members participate in university extension courses and pool their experience and talents to create learning and social programs for themselves.

Study groups and workshops evolve out of the interests of the members. Ongoing study groups explore such subjects as literature, opera, languages, creative writing, singing, art history, ecology, human potential, and gardening. Social activities, including walking tours through the Bay Area and impromptu parties, are also available.

Members pay an annual fee of $100, which entitles them to participate in all CLIR activities and to enroll in extension courses to the full value of this membership fee.

San Francisco State University

Sixty-Plus
1600 Holloway Avenue
San Francisco, CA 94132
Marnie St. Clair, Division of Continuing Education

Retired and semiretired men and women of the Bay Area are invited to join with their contemporaries in the Sixty-Plus program. Benefits include: biweekly lectures and discussion with university professors and other qualified speakers from the community; one-day, and on occasion, weekend tours; social sessions following meetings and observer status in university courses.

University of San Francisco

Institute for Life-Long Learning
San Francisco, CA 94117
Ralph Lane, Jr., Department of Sociology

Through the Fromm Institute for Life-Long Learning, persons 50 years old and over may enroll for an unlimited number of campus courses for an annual tuition of $150.

University of Southern California

Andrus Volunteer Program
Ethel Percy Andrus Gerontology Center
University Park
Los Angeles, CA 90007
Polly McConney, Director

Unlike most college programs *for* older adults, this is a program *of* older adults for the university, specifically the Andrus Gerontology Center, one of the most important in the country.

The Andrus volunteers are one hundred men and women from all over the Los Angeles area. They range in age from 50 to 80 and bring to their various projects a wide variety of experience from professional, business, and volunteer service backgrounds. The objective of the volunteer program is to advance the research, education, and service goals of the gerontology center.

Specifically, they serve as both research subjects and research designers; conduct tours and act as docents; serve as peer counselors; design and plan seminars on aging and volunteerism for older people in the Los Angeles area; serve in a variety of roles at multipurpose senior centers, and publish a newsletter to foster communication among staff, students, and volunteers. They are the writers/editors of two books, available through the Gerontology Center, *Releasing the Potential of the Older Volunteer* (see page 85) and *Aging: Today's Research and You.*

California State College at Dominguez Hills

Dominguez Hills, CA 90747
Herman J. Loether, Department of
Sociology

The Social Systems Research Center of the Sociology Department has developed an intergenerational learning experience where students ranging in age from their teens to over 70 work together. Older people from the community are invited to work with fellow students on research projects to earn college credit.

University of California at San Diego

Institute for Continued Learning
University Extension Q-014
La Jolla, CA 92093
Doris R. Brosnan, Director

The Institute for Continued Learning provides peer group teaching, educational programs, and cultural activities for older adults. The annual membership is $75 per person or $125 per couple. Each member is required to take at least one ICL study group session course and one extension course during the enrollment period.

Social activities, use of the university library, lectures, a craft center, low-cost charter flights, and other benefits go with the membership.

California Lutheran College

Lifelong Learning Program
60 Olsen Road
Thousand Oaks, CA 91360
R. W. Edmund, Director

Retired persons are invited to volunteer their services as teachers or staff. In return, the college offers free tuition for all courses and in some cases furnishes housing.

Santa Monica College

Emeritus College
1815 Pearl Street
Santa Monica, CA 90405
Marilyn H. Hall, Director

Approximately seventy-five courses are offered in each eight-week period. The program reaches about 1200–1300 people, with a total enrollment of 3500. Courses are offered in many locations throughout the community, during daylight hours. A donation of $2 a course is typical.

Connecticut
University of Connecticut

Human Development Center
U-Box 117
Storrs, CT 06268
Howard A. Rosencranz, Director

A number of programs specifically for older adults are offered, including twice-weekly swimming and exercise, nutrition education, and Experts Emeritus, a five-week session of evening courses.

Florida
Nova University

Institute for Retired Professionals
Institute for Lifelong Awareness
3301 College Avenue
Fort Lauderdale, FL 33314
Lloyd D. Elgart, Director

Modeled after the Institute for Retired Professionals at New York's New School for Social Research (see pages 42–44), Nova's IRP is designed to meet the particular needs and circumstances of the south Florida retired person. The program offers a new opportunity for highly trained retired professionals to renew their education at the university level without the usual course procedures. Because of the varied interests and experiences of the retired community, members act as both teachers and students.

Another Nova University program is the Institute for Lifelong Awareness, founded in the belief that growth should be a lifelong process. The institute serves the community, young and old, with a wide variety of noncredit workshops, lecture series, and seminars. Special activities and events are offered in the fields of the arts and travel.

Eckerd College
   Academy for Senior Professionals
   St. Petersburg, FL 33733
   Dr. Clark H. Bouwman, Director

This is another program modeled on the New School's Institute for Retired Professionals (see pages 42–44). Classes are designed as forums and led by moderators, not instructors. Depending on the length of the semester, members pay from $30 to $50 for each forum, with the privilege of three guest visits to each of the other forums. Members may also audit regular college courses for a reduced fee. Since the program is relatively new, it is experimenting with a number of new approaches.

Georgia
Georgia State University
   University Plaza
   Atlanta, GA 30303

The university is involved in a new effort to attract retired people back to the campus. A back-to-college seminar assists the older student make the transition from the work or retirement role into the academic community.

In the Continuing Education program, noncredit seminars are held periodically for people in the field of gerontology and for older individuals on such topics as family relationships, the economics of independent living, drug use, pre-retirement planning, and legal problems.

Illinois
Southern Illinois University
   Box 121
   Edwardsville, IL 62026
   Dr. Anthony J. Traxler, Director,
      Gerontology Program

Various departments and schools throughout the university are actively seeking the admission of older adults and have developed special programs and support systems for the mature student. The Gerontology Program and the General Studies Division co-sponsor monthly workshops for older persons desiring career counseling, retraining, a college education, or continuing education. The Gerontology Program also sponsors public-service programs for older adults free of charge: "Dialogue with Senior Citizens," a cultural and educational improvement program for older adults; an annual Senior Citizens Fair; and various workshops and noncredit courses. An "Educard Program" permits older adults to attend classes throughout the university on a noncredit basis for a fee of $10 per quarter.

Iowa
Westmar College
   JANUS Program
   Le Mars, IA 51031

JANUS is a residential program for persons aged 50 and older, who live in campus apartments or residence halls, eating in the dining room, taking courses for credit or audit, and attending any campus events. The program also includes commuting students.

Kansas
Tabor College
   Hillsboro, KS 67063

Older adults participate in the college's Senior Student Day, held each Friday, which includes lunch in the cafeteria, participating in a life-enrichment series, and selecting one or more courses designed particularly for older students. Members of this 60+ Program may also audit regular courses free of charge.

Kentucky
University of Kentucky
   Council on Aging
   Lexington, KY 40506
   C. R. Hager, Director

The Council on Aging, set up in 1962, administers the Donovan Fellowship program and the Writing Workshop for People Over 57.

More than 200 students are enrolled each semester in the Donovan Fellowship program, which permits people over 65 to enroll in regular university courses, without tuition, either for credit or noncredit. Donovan scholars, as they are called, come from every walk of life and almost every state of the union, including Hawaii. Many of them work toward a degree. In addition to the regular courses, there are special courses and forums for the Donovan scholars.

The summer Writing Workshop for People Over 57 is held each August and always filled to capacity. Fifty-seven was chosen, in case you are wondering, because it is halfway between the age of 65, when most people retire, and 50, when they may start thinking about retirement.

Maryland
Loyola College
4501 North Charles Street
Baltimore, MD 21210
Sr. Mary Cleophas Costello, Director

"Creative Living" for adults who are 55 and over consists of lectures by faculty members from a variety of departments, in which they talk about new developments in their fields. A social hour and question period follows, and members may also audit regular courses for a fee of $25 per course.

Salisbury State College
Institute for Retired Persons
Salisbury, MD 21801
Harold O. Schaffer, Director

Although it is modeled on the New School's Institute for Retired Professionals (see pages 42–44), the Salisbury IRP, as its name indicates, is open to professionals and nonprofessionals alike. Anyone over the age of 50, retired or semiretired, is welcome to participate. For a membership fee of $10 a semester, members may attend Friday afternoon forums, participate in seminars,

and attend classes. The motto of the IRP is, "It's not too late to be everything you want to be or do everything you want to do."

Massachusetts
Harvard University
Institute for Learning in Retirement
B-3 Lehman Hall
Cambridge, MA 02138

The core of the Institute for Learning in Retirement program is a variety of study groups based on cooperative leadership and membership participation. The groups operate on a volunteer peer-teaching principle. Members are thus students and teachers simultaneously. A typical study group meets for two hours one day a week throughout the term. Class participants assume the responsibility of presenting reports and papers at the sessions.

Members of the institute are also eligible to enroll in the credit courses offered by the Harvard Extension School and the noncredit courses of the Center for Continuing Education. "The Medieval Town," a study trip to Oxford University, was planned for the summer of 1978.

Membership applications are reviewed by an admissions committee, which selects members from a variety of careers and educational backgrounds. In addition to people in full or semiretirement, applications are accepted from those approaching retirement who have the time to participate in the program. Only a limited number of new members can be admitted each year. The annual membership fee is $150.

Southeastern Massachusetts University
Institute on Health and Long Life
North Dartmouth, MA 02747
Robert Lewis Piper, Division of Continuing Studies

The Institute on Health and Long Life seeks to attract older and other students to deal with the theoretical and practical concerns of older adults. No tuition is charged for persons 59 and older. Extensive training programs are offered.

Michigan
Aquinas College
Emeritus College
Grand Rapids, MI 49506
Sister Agnes Thiel, Director

Emeritus College is a seminar program for "the fifty-plus generation." The seminars, held in an informal setting, offer the opportunity for reading and discussion on a variety of topics. There are no papers or exams and previous college experience is not necessary. The cost is $10 for a four-session seminar, or $3 for a single session.

Minnesota
College of Saint Benedict
Intergenerational Living/Learning
  Program
St. Joseph, MN 56734
Sister Justin Feeley, Director

Women of all ages, with special invitations to those over 60, participate in the intergenerational programs. The core aspects of the program are a weekly seminar, weekend programs focusing on key topics, and live-in programs during January and the summer months. No special requirements.

New Hampshire
New England College
Pioneers Program
Henniker, NH 03242
James Verschueren, Director

Modeled after the Elderhostel program (see pages 37–42), Pioneers offers courses in two-week modules. There are three two-week sessions each spring and fall and a person seeking college credit for a course would sign up for the full six weeks (although each module is a complete mini-course in itself). Students range in age from 55 to 80-plus, and while they are encouraged to live on campus, most of them, so far, live in the area. The Pioneers Program

was started in the academic year 1977–1978. Courses for the first year included environmental literacy, lifespan psychology, communicating with an audience, business and ethics, raku pottery, and music appreciation. Cost per module is $100. Room and board is $90.

New Jersey
Fairleigh Dickinson University— Madison
Educational Program for Older Persons
285 Madison Avenue
Madison, NJ 07940
Joseph L. Tramutola, Jr., Director

The Educational Program for Older Persons has been in operation since 1972 and offers innovative social and educational opportunities, tuition free, to the older citizen 65 and over.

Audit undergraduate and graduate courses are available as well as participation in many social activities. The Division of Life Experience offers specially designed courses for older students.

Fairleigh Dickinson University— Teaneck
Women's Outreach Program
1000 River Road
Teaneck, NJ 07666
Dan Grodofsky, Department of Social
  Work

The Women's Outreach Program, which includes change of career, study skills, and other seminars, is offered to entering students at no charge. An Invitation to Humanities Program is open to all adults 65 and over. An interdisciplinary concentration in aging, providing a wide variety of courses, is being offered.

New York
New School for Social Research
Institute for Retired Professionals
66 West 12th Street
New York, NY 10011
(See description on pages 42–44.)

A Pioneer student in music appreciation class at New England College in Henniker, New Hampshire. *Photo credit: Bruce Levin*

Fordham University

The College at Sixty
Lincoln Center
113 West 60th Street
New York, NY 10023
(See description on pages 44–46.)

Brooklyn College of the City University of New York

Institute for Retired Professionals and
  Executives
Adult Education Department
Bedford Avenue and Avenue H
Brooklyn, NY 11210

The Brooklyn College IRP opened in the fall of 1977 with one study group and a handful of interested people. Within a year the number of classes had risen to eighteen, with 250 members. The program is modeled after the New School's IRP (see pages 42–44). Membership is $25 a person or $40 a couple.

Pace University

Active Retirement Center
School of Continuing Education
Pace Plaza
New York, NY 10038
Abbie Jean Brownell, Director

Adults over 55 may become members of the Active Retirement Center, which functions at Pace's three campuses. The center provides, at special rates, credit courses, auditing courses, special courses, activities, a placement service, and pre-retirement counseling.

The Executive Emeritus Council functions on the Pleasantville campus as a part of the Active Retirement Center. It is made up of retired executives, who act as advisers, consultants, and speakers, as needed. One member of the council acts as coordinator of the program.

Older women may participate in the New Directions for Women program, which is located at the New York City campus.

Hofstra University
Professionals and Executives in
  Retirement (PEIR)
Division of Continuing Education
Hempstead, NY 11550
Rose Spitz, Director

Hofstra's Center for Professionals and Executives in Retirement—with its access to the university's wealth of cultural offerings in the sciences, humanities, libraries, galleries, theater, and music—is modeled after the New School's IRP (see pages 42–44). PEIR members design the curriculum and choose the activities and projects they wish to join. Study groups and special "action projects" are developed by teams of two or three members.

For an annual fee of $225, PEIR members may enroll in one Hofstra noncredit course each semester, and take as many PIER courses as they wish. Membership is by application and interview.

North Carolina
Duke University
Institute for Learning in Retirement
107 Bivens Building
Durham, NC 27708

Institute members design, teach, and administer their own activities, which include courses, field trips, discussion groups, counseling, and community service. Courses range from a seminar on modern China to "What's Happening to Ourselves?" which covers issues ranging from sexuality to social security.

Membership is by application and interview and is limited to retired people interested in stimulating intellectual activity. The tuition fee is $8 per month.

Ohio
Ohio State University
Program 60
1947 College Road
Columbus, OH 43210
Harold Schneiderman, School of Social
  Work

Program 60 offers a variety of services and opportunities to older adults. Among them: Project Reminiscing, in which journalism students interview older citizens of the community; serving as volunteers in the student union and as assistants to the registrar during the quarterly registration periods; and serving as jurors in Moot Court to help students in law school practice jury selection. The program offers free enrollment in university courses, on a space-available basis and with no course credit.

Case Western Reserve University
Institute for Retirement Studies
2040 Adelbert Road
Cleveland, OH 44106
James G. Taafe, Director

The Institute for Retirement Studies is an academic program and retirement planning unit for persons 50 and over. For a membership fee of $25 a semester, university courses may be audited or taken for credit toward a degree. Students may attend part or full time, but must register for a minimum of one course a year. The institute also offers its own noncredit courses, taught by university faculty and open only to institute members.

(Note: The Retirement Planning Program provides professional service to business, industry, and other organizations in the area of pre-retirement preparation. It trains personnel to develop and carry out in-house retirement planning.)

Kent State University
Gerontology Center
Continuing Education
Kent, OH 44240
Susan W. Ritchie, Director

Under the Senior Guest Student program, retired adults over 50 may audit classes on a tuition-free, space-available basis. If you are over 60, under Ohio law, you may do so whether or not you are retired. All Senior Guest students may, if they like, participate in the Gateway Seminar for one quarter before starting classes. The administration considers this an extremely helpful way of easing an older student into the campus environment. It also provides a setting for fellowship and shared experience with other Senior Guest students.

Oregon
University of Oregon

Division of Developmental Studies and
  Services
Oregon Center for Gerontology
1627 Agate Street
Eugene, OR 97403
Frances G. Scott, Director

Persons aged 65 or older not seeking credit and not working toward a degree may attend classes free on a space-available basis. There may be charges for special materials. Older adults are encouraged to attend gerontology classes on this basis. In addition, retired persons from the immediate vicinity of the university are given opportunities to serve as volunteers working with gerontology students on an individual basis, thus contributing to the student's education and knowledge of the aging process.

Portland State University

Institute on Aging
Multidisciplinary Center of Gerontology
Portland, OR 97207
Douglas G. Montgomery

Retired Associates offers retired professional people the opportunity to participate in a full range of university activities on a club membership basis. Counseling for Older Individuals is a program operated by the student counseling service of the university. It provides specially trained counselors to work with older adults who are considering midcareer or post-retirement shifts in lifestyle or orientation. The League of Older Students provides a fraternitylike membership organization for older students who are pursuing a degree. The league gives them the opportunity to come together for common purpose and mutual support as they pursue career development in later life.

Pennsylvania
Temple University

Association for Retired Professionals
1619 Walnut Street
Philadelphia, PA 19103
Frank Tooke, Director

"A brain-saver" is how a former department store executive describes the Association for Retired Professionals. Modeled after the New School's IRP (see pages 42–44), the association had 475 members in 1978.

Membership is open to retired people whose education, experience, and previous activities "have led them to a need and desire for further adult continuing education and enrichment." Most of the members have attended college and a majority have earned at least one degree; however, many are high-school graduates with distinguished life experience. The program is not a special course created by Temple University for retired people, but rather one developed by the members themselves with the help and encouragement of the university.

Many of the courses, workshops, and seminars are conducted by the members, who are retired from a remarkable diversity of jobs in teaching, the law, government, science, journalism, the arts, industry, and business. In addition, ARP members may audit courses throughout the university.

Membership is by application and interview. The annual fee is $50.

Bucknell University
Cross-Generational Program
Lewisburg, PA 17837
Douglas K. Candland, Department of
Psychology

Older adults are eligible to participate in the Cross-Generational Program, a living and learning project that sponsors social, cultural, and intellectual events for students and older people.

The university is also developing an Alternative Employment Opportunities Project, designed to encourage people who have been mandatorily retired to seek out and develop alternative employment.

Indiana University of Pennsylvania
Older Americans Program
Uhler Hall
Indiana, PA 15701
Brian J. McCue, School of Continuing
Education

The Older Americans Program offers educational, cultural, and recreational opportunities as well as referral and information services for those older people who are not being reached by existing programs. In addition, there is a Morning with the Professors Program, a series of lectures offered for noncredit at half the regular fee. The university also offers a wide variety of other noncredit courses, including ones of special interest to older people, through the Community-University Studies Program.

Mercyhurst College
College of Older Americans
501 E. 38th Street
Erie, PA 16501
Cyprian J. Cooney, Department of
Sociology

The College of Older Americans provides direct educational service programs to persons aged 40 and over. These include special six-week minicourses in all areas of the liberal arts at $10 per course, as well as the auditing of regular courses. Approximately fifty persons are enrolled each term in the COA.

South Dakota
Augustana College
The TELL Institute
1600 S. Minnesota Avenue
Sioux Falls, SD 57105
L. Milton Erickson, Community
Education

The TELL Institute is a joint project of Augustana College, Community College, North American Baptist Seminary, and Sioux Falls College. It offers workshops and courses designed to enrich later life through retirement planning, older American education, and gerontological studies. Tuition ranges from none to $20, depending upon the course.

Huron College
Huron, SD 57350
Karen L. Hornung, Department of
Gerontology and Adult Education

Under a program entitled Developing Adult Resources through Education, the college and senior center are offering forty noncredit courses to approximately 400 people.

Washington
Central Washington University
In-Residence Senior Scholars Program
Ellensburg, WA 98926
Elwyn H. Odell, Department of Political
Science

The university has an In-Residence Senior Scholars Program for people 55 and over, at regular fees. Students take seven hours of courses per quarter, or equivalent hours in services of various kinds to college programs in which they have knowledge or skills, or a combination of classes and service.

Fairhaven College
　The Bridge Project
　Bellingham, WA 98225
　(See description on pages 46–48.)

Wisconsin
University of Wisconsin at Whitewater
　Live-In-and-Learn Program
　Whitewater, WI 53190
　This is the program whose best-known

students were a 70-year-old daughter and her 93-year-old mother. Older people may live in dormitories for $75 a month and either pay for food in the cafeteria or cook in their rooms. Tuition at all Wisconsin state universities is free for people over 62 who audit classes. Although the live-in part of the program has been slow to catch on, about one hundred older people attend classes while living at home.

Institutes of Lifetime Learning

More than fifty Extension Institutes of Lifetime Learning, sponsored by Retired Teachers Association units and American Association of Retired Persons chapters throughout the country, offer programs and courses geared to the needs of older persons. Many are co-sponsored by local institutions of post-secondary education, such as the University of Akron, Southern Colorado State College, and San Antonio Union Junior College.

The institutes' two original centers, located in Washington, D.C., and Long Beach, California, also sponsor programs in cooperation with local educational institutions.

In conjunction with the graduate school of the U.S. Department of Agriculture (a continuing education facility), the Washington Institute provides courses for more than 500 older persons each semester. Classes at the Long Beach Institute are also offered in cooperation with local educational institutions.

Older persons and other community representatives take an active role in the extensions by serving on advisory boards. In some cases, extension classes are taught by retired educators in the community.

Extension courses are minimally priced, nongraded, and offered during daytime hours at convenient locations. For information, write the national office or the chairman in your area.

The Institute of Lifetime Learning
　NRTA-AARP
　1909 K Street, N.W.
　Washington, DC 20049

Alabama
Tuscaloosa Extension
　Frank Kendall, Chairman

　3821 2nd Avenue
　Tuscaloosa, AL 35401

Arkansas
Horseshoe Bend Extension
　Harold Plank, Chairman
　1211 Orchard Lane
　Horseshoe Bend, AR 72512

Garland County Extension
Edwin C. Doulin, Chairman
104 E. Britt Lane
Hot Springs, AR 71901

California
The Institute of Lifetime Learning
NRTA-AARP
215 Long Beach Boulevard
Long Beach, CA 90801

California City Extension
Mrs. Ina A. deWilde, Chairman
274 Desert Breeze Drive
California City, CA 93505

Southern Inyo Extension
Mrs. Margaret T. Saunders
P.O. Box 865
Lone Pine, CA 93545

Oakland Extension
Ralph R. Pletcher, Chairman
9 Rydal Court
Oakland, CA 94611

Ontario-Upland Extension
Mrs. Felicia DeLuise
1225 Eddington Street
Ontario, CA 91786

Colorado
Pueblo Extension
Dr. Rudolf Lassner, Chairman
124 Baylor
Pueblo, CO 81005

District of Columbia
Washington, D.C., Extension
Ms. Patricia Hickson, Program
    Coordinator
U.S. Department of Agriculture
Washington, DC 20250

Florida
Sarasota Extension
Mrs. Marguerite Allen, Chairman
4330 Falmouth Drive, Apt. 204
Longboat Key, FL 33548

St. Petersburg Extension
Mrs. Genevieve Blinn, Chairman
5998 Grove Street
St. Petersburg, FL 33705

Central Florida Extension
Oswald Knapp, Jr., Chairman
1214 Turner Road
Winter Park, FL 32789

Illinois
Metro-East Area Extension
William Cassiday, Chairman
430 Belleview
Alton, IL 62002

Metro-East Area Extension
Ms. Penny Neale, Program Coordinator
Belleville Area College-Uptown Center
Belleville, IL 62221

Metro-East Area Extension
Jerome Bradley, Program Coordinator
Lewis and Clark Community College
Godfrey, IL 62035

Metro-East Extension
Clyde Fisher, Program Coordinator
Office of Off-Campus Programs
Southern Illinois University
Edwardsville, IL 62026

Greater Chicago Extension
Ms. Ruth Gallinot, Program Coordinator
Central YMCA Community College
211 W. Wacker Drive
Chicago, IL 60606

West Suburban Extension
Mrs. Marie Gustafson, Chairman
565 Swain Street
Elmhurst, IL 60126

Iowa
Iowa City Area Extension
Lester Benz, Chairman
2315 Rochester Avenue
Iowa City, IA 52240

Louisiana
Oakdale Extension
    Mrs. V. M. Martin, Chairman
    P.O. Box 475
    Oakdale, LA 71463

Minnesota
Southwest Minnesota Extension
    Mrs. L. W. Archbold, Chairman
    515 E. College Drive
    Marshall, MN 56258

Minneapolis Area Extension
    E. H. Stock, Chairman
    10716 Morris Avenue South
    Minneapolis, MN 55437

Missouri
Mid-America Extension
    Dr. Susan Imel, Program Coordinator
    Avila College
    11901 Wornall Road
    Kansas City, MO 64145

Montana
Gallatin Park Area Extension
    Kenneth Harman, Chairman
    1407 S. 3rd Avenue
    Bozeman, MT 59715

Nebraska
Columbus Extension
    Ms. Mabel Hadcock, Chairman
    1704 14th Street
    Columbus, NE 68601

New Jersey
Northern New Jersey Extension
    Mrs. Carmen Lagos Signes, Chairman
    299 E. 31st Street
    Paterson, NJ 07504

Northern New Jersey Extension
    Ms. Kathy Manko, Program Coordinator
    Department of Adult Continuing
        Education
    Montclair State College
    Upper Montclair, NJ 07043

New York
Queensborough Extension
    Mrs. Barbara Pennipede, Chairman
    Queensborough College
    56th Avenue and Springfield
    Bayside, NY 11364

Lehman Extension
    Dr. George E. Brown, Chairman
    Herbert H. Lehman College
    Bedford Park Boulevard West
    Bronx, NY 10468

Greater Manhasset Extension
    Mrs. Hildegarde Stoeltzing, Chairman
    10 Stratford Road
    Port Washington, NY 11050

Plattsburgh Extension
    Ralph G. Hoag, Chairman
    5 Lynde Street
    Plattsburgh, NY 12901

North Carolina
Macon County Extension
    Mrs. Kitty Swanson, Chairman
    15 Ivar Street
    Franklin, NC 28734

Ohio
Akron Regional Extension
    Leroy E. Dietz, Chairman
    682 Sherman Street
    Akron, OH 44311

Baldwin-Wallace Extension
    Mrs. Carmella Cehelsky, Chairman
    3552 Granton Avenue
    Cleveland, OH 44111

Canton Regional Extension
    Grant Stanley, Chairman
    812 Rose Lane Street, S.W.
    North Canton, OH 44720

Oklahoma
Grove Extension
    Al Hummel, Chairman
    Route 3, Lake Park Village
    Grove, OK 74344

Oregon

Bend Extension
Dr. Jerome Benson, Chairman
111 Kings Lane
Romaine Village
Bend, OR 97701

South Dakota

Institute for Enrichment of Later Life
John Nelson, Chairman
1200 W. 28th Street
Sioux Falls, SD 57105

Texas

Austin Extension
Dr. Walter Pilgrim, Program
  Coordinator
709 E. 46th Street
Austin, TX 78751

Corpus Christi Extension
Mrs. Flora Pockrus, Chairman
1914 Hawthorne
Corpus Christi, TX 78404

Dallas-Walnut Hill Extension
Dr. Arthur L. Harding, Chairman
6426 Park Lane
Dallas, TX 75225

Houston Extension
Dr. Noble B. Armstrong, Chairman
830 Rosewick Street
Houston, TX 77015

Odessa Extension
Mrs. Thelma Newman, Chairman
Box 1284
Odessa, TX 79760

Rockport Extension
Dr. J. F. Benjamin, Chairman
1414 Paisano Street
Rockport, TX 78382

San Antonio Extension
A. M. Borchers, Chairman
609 Westwood Drive
San Antonio, TX 78212

Victoria Area Extension
Ms. Ara L. Sumney, Chairman
1007 Melrose
Victoria, TX 77901

McLennan County Extension
James Lilly, Chairman
1400 College Drive
Waco, TX 76708

Virginia

Richmond Extension
Dr. Spencer Albright, Chairman
5611 Three Chopt Road
Richmond, VA 23226

Washington

Yakima Extension
Mrs. Gladys Heit, Program Coordinator
2120 S. 5th Avenue
Yakima, WA 98902

Wisconsin

Fox Valley Extension
Herbert H. Helble, Chairman
838 E. North Street
Appleton, WI 54911

Tri-County Extension
Ms. Alma J. Klug, Chairman
2616 75th Street
Kenosha, WI 53140

CHAPTER 5

Volunteer Opportunities

One area in which older people can find virtually unlimited, useful, and interesting opportunities is that of volunteering. Many necessary services to children, the elderly, and the general community would go unfilled without volunteer workers, especially those with the time to work on a fairly regular basis. The national programs described in this chapter are, perhaps, only the most interesting tip of the iceberg—local city halls, church groups, school systems, and community agencies also have lists of needed volunteer jobs.

Almost by definition, volunteer programs do not pay any salaries, although a few, such as the Peace Corps, VISTA, and the International Executive Service Corps, do pay expenses and readjustment allowances. The Foster Grandparent Program and the Senior Companions program, however, are for low-income volunteers and do pay a small salary.

Foster Grandparent Program

Almost 16,000 low-income people over 60 are volunteer workers in this fifteen-year-old federal program that marries the needs of older adults to earn some money in a useful way with the needs of handicapped children for love and attention. Most of the foster grandparents work in institutions where they provide companionship and guidance to children with emotional, physical, or mental handicaps. Recently, however, the program has been expanded in some areas to work with children in their own homes.

In Pittsburgh, twelve foster grandparents are working directly with thirty-three families where there are problems of child abuse and neglect, alcoholism, and emotional and physical illness. Their aim is to keep family units together and prevent institutionalization. The grandparents serve as "stabilizing components" in otherwise unstable households, explained the director, Shirley Arch. A unique aspect of this program is that besides supporting the children in the family, the grandparents "parent the parents" by modeling good parent behavior to adults who in many cases simply do not know how to care for their children correctly.

Each day that the grandparent is in the home, the parent (usually the mother) must be present to learn from the grandparent such things as how to deal with a child other than by using physical measures; how to stimulate children mentally with reading flash cards, or how to develop physical coordination with building toys. The foster grandparents are taught the best type of intervention while in the home, in-

A Foster Grandparent with the dollhouse he built for his little girl at the State Hospital and Training School in Winfield, Kansas.

cluding, for example, playing with the children in order to relieve some of the pressure on the parent.

With the help of instructors from Penn State and the University of Pittsburgh, the volunteers are taught family therapy techniques. Among other things, they learn the pattern that occurs from generation to generation in which neglectful parents are the children of neglectful parents. Although there are no educational requirements to become a foster grandparent, the program is in itself an education. Initial training consists of a forty-hour orientation course, but training is ongoing. Each week, the grandparents in the program attend a full-day session with a psychologist in rehabilitation counseling. Orientation programs and in-service training are a part of all the Foster Grandparent programs.

Foster grandparents work twenty hours a week and are paid $1.60 an hour. They are reimbursed for transportation and receive a meal each day that they work.

ACTION, the federal agency that administers the Foster Grandparent Program, has regional offices in Boston, New York, Philadelphia, Atlanta, Chicago, Dallas, Kansas City, Denver, San Francisco, and Seattle. Look up the address and telephone number under U.S. Government, or write or call, toll-free:

ACTION
806 Connecticut Avenue, N.W.
Washington, DC 20525
800-424-8580

Senior Companions

Newer and smaller than the Foster Grandparent Program, the Senior Companions are also low-income people aged 60 and over, who give individualized care and companionship to frail elderly people at home or in institutions. With the support of a Senior Companion, many elderly people who otherwise would have to go to nursing homes can remain in their own homes, living semi-independent existences. There are fewer than 3000 Senior Companions who serve 6000 elderly people.

Pay and benefits are the same as for the Foster Grandparent Program.

For further information, see ACTION, above.

Peace Corps

When the President's mother, "Miss Lillian" Carter, joined the Peace Corps at 68, she was unusual but not unique. At last count, there were

A Mississippi Foster Grandparent reads to his two small boys.

6850 volunteers serving in sixty-two countries; 306 of them were between the ages of 51 and 70, and 29 were between 71 and 80.

Peace Corps volunteers work in Latin America, Africa, Asia, and the Pacific. They offer skills in a variety of programs: maternal and child health, family nutrition, fresh-water fisheries, agriculture, teacher training, mathematics and science education, vocational education, small business consulting, public administration, and natural resource development and conservation.

The term of service is generally two years. Qualifications are U.S. citizenship and good health.

Transportation is provided to training sites and overseas assignments (including transportation for home leave in the event of family emergencies) and volunteers receive a monthly allowance for rent, food, travel, and all medical needs. A readjustment allowance of $125 a month is set aside, payable on completion of service.

For information, see ACTION, above.

VISTA (Volunteers in Service to America)

Almost 50,000 VISTA members live and work among the poor, serving for one year in urban and rural areas and on Indian reservations. They are assigned to community organizations and social service agencies in the United States, Puerto Rico, the Virgin Islands, and Guam. About half of the volunteers are low-income persons; 15 percent are 55 or older.

Although good health is a requirement, a physical handicap does not disqualify a volunteer provided placement can be made on a VISTA project.

Service is in the fields of community organization, education, health, drug abuse, corrections, day care, legal aid, architectural design, city planning, and weatherization.

Volunteers receive a basic living allowance to cover housing and food and $75 a month is paid as a stipend upon completion of service. The VISTA allowance does not affect social security or welfare payments, but it is subject to taxes.

For information, see ACTION, above.

RSVP (Retired Senior Volunteer Program)

All of the volunteers in this, the largest of the programs under AC-TION, are retired or semiretired persons 60 and over. At present there are more than 235,000 volunteers serving in almost 700 programs.

The range of services is as wide as the needs, but two directives to local stations make this program particularly meaningful for the older volunteer who wants more than the satisfaction of doing good. The assignments must be "directed to the interests, skills, needs, and physical limitations of the volunteer" and they must "be in the company of other people or other RSVP volunteers when possible." In other words, you should find an RSVP assignment both interesting and sociable.

Among the agencies served by RSVP volunteers are courts, schools, libraries, day-care centers, hospitals, nursing homes, economic development agencies, and other community service centers. A retired black cowboy has talked about his life to youngsters in a Chicago museum. In Fort Worth, Texas, volunteers are assisting the public library in compiling a history of blacks in Texas from the Depression Era to the present. Armed with tape recorders, they are interviewing both black and white residents.

In Tampa, Florida, where the number of elderly poor people comprise an unusually large portion of the population, Law, Inc., a free legal-aid service, wanted to form a senior advocacy unit. They did so with nine RSVP volunteers, each of whom works in a special area. A retired accountant handles the medicare and insurance claims. A retired labor negotiator performs outreach services at local nutrition sites. Other members of the unit are a former professor of logic, two retired businessmen, a social worker, and a woman who graduated from college at 63 (before going on to get her Ph.D. in adult education and writing a book on consumer problems of the elderly). Since the RSVP unit was formed in 1976, the legal-aid service has been able to reach a significantly larger number of the elderly in the Tampa area.

The Willoughby-Eastlake City School District in Lake County, Ohio, which ran a one-year pilot program using RSVP volunteers in the schools, has published a guide to involving schools with older volunteers. One case history, in particular, points up the benefits to both old and young in the senior volunteer program.

K's wife had read about our program in the schools in our local newspaper.

She called us and asked, "Would your school's RSVP accept a blind man?"

She went on to say that her husband was a wonderful man, a retired machinist who had retained his ability to repair machines through the sense of touch. She added that he had just finished repairing her washing machine, and that neighbors were always asking him to help them in repairing household appliances. She said, however, that he was becoming bored with too many empty hours to fill by listening to the radio and visiting senior centers.

We told her that we would check back with her in a day. The next step was a visit to one of our local junior high schools where they had requested a volunteer in the industrial training center.

We were doubtful about the reception the principal would give us; however we thought all we could do was ask, and if he said no, we would try to place our blind volunteer in some other kind of station.

The school principal and the industrial arts teacher both decided that they would like to try this as an experiment, even though we explained that his wife would accompany K. She said she would lead him to the classroom and take him to the lunchroom.

This was the beginning of the school year, and the young people in this class were ninth-graders. They were learning to take motors apart and put them back together again. They watched in amazement as K felt the motors and told them the approximate year the motors were made.

At the end of the week, the students informed Mrs. K that her presence was no longer necessary; they would have someone waiting when K was dropped off, they would escort him to the lunchroom and would see him to the car when he was through with his volunteer work.

K spends three afternoons a week in the school. He has given the young people he is working with and the teachers so much more than his knowledge about motors. He has proved that a handicap need not sour a disposition or bar anyone from active involvement with others.

K assists with a class both before and after the lunch break. Originally after finishing his lunch, he would wait in the teachers' lounge until time for his second class. The kids soon put a stop to that. They decided that they would take turns reading the daily newspaper or books to K.

In every way the youngsters and teachers at that school show their spontaneous love and admiration for K. For his birthday, they gave him a party. Several times, when his wife had to be away from home, they arranged with her that they could come into his home and prepare surprise dinner parties for him. At the close of the first school year, the students presented him with a shop jacket with the school insignia.

For information about RSVP, see ACTION, above.

Legal Services to the Elderly

A major program to expand free legal services to the elderly poor in all areas of the country will succeed only with the help of many thousands of older volunteers who will work as paralegals. Operating under the Administration on Aging, each state now has a Legal Services Developer charged with setting up and staffing the programs. To volunteer your services, write or call the office in your own state, listed below. As an estimate of how many volunteers will be needed, Mr. J. J. Donovan, of the Department of Elder Affairs of Massachusetts, says that his state will need more than 500 volunteers throughout the state.

A legal background is not necessary. Volunteers will receive training and work under the supervision of attorneys.

A few part-time paying jobs are available for low-income people who qualify. See Senior Aides in chapter 7.

Alabama

John Henig
Commission on Aging
740 Madison Avenue
Montgomery, AL 36130
205-832-6640

Alaska

Elizabeth Ratner
Alaska Legal Services
1 West 6th Avenue
Anchorage, AK 99501
907-272-9431

Arizona

John Vanlandingham
Bureau of Aging
Department of Economic Security
1400 W. Washington
Phoenix, AZ 85004
602-271-4446

Arkansas

Brady Anderson
Office on Aging
Seventh and Gaines Streets
P.O. Box 2179
Little Rock, AR 72203
501-371-2441

California

Dan Silva
Department of Aging
918 J Street
Sacramento, CA 95814
916-322-6715

Colorado

Gene Reisdorff
Division of Services for the Aging
Department of Social Services
1575 Sherman Street, Room 506
Denver, CO 80203
303-892-3673

Connecticut

Norman Johnson
Department on Aging
90 Washington Street, Room 312
Hartford, CT 06115
203-566-7725

Delaware

Nick Kakaroukas
Division of Aging
Department of Health and Social
   Services
2413 Lancaster Avenue
Wilmington, DE 19805
302-571-3481

District of Columbia

Eileen Mann
Legal Counsel for the Elderly
1016 16th Street, N.W., 6th Floor
Washington, DC 20036
202-234-0970

Florida

Andrea Wood
Office of Aging Services
Department of Health and
   Rehabilitation Services
1323 Winewood Boulevard
Tallahassee, FL 32301
904-488-2881

Georgia

Thom Dowen
Office of Aging
Department of Human Resources
618 Ponce de Leon, N.E.
Atlanta, GA 30308
404-894-5333

Hawaii

Dennis Ihara
Executive Office on Aging
1149 Bethel Street, Room 307
Honolulu, HI 96513
808-548-2593

Idaho

Debbie Bail
Senior Adults Law Project
104½ S. Capitol
Boise, ID 83706
208-345-0106

Illinois

George Mittleman
Department on Aging
910 S. Michigan Avenue, Room 508
Chicago, IL 60605
312-793-2914

Driving a Car

Changes in vision that occur naturally with aging should not prevent older Americans from involvement in community activities, according to the American Optometric Association.

One of the most common fallacies is that the elderly must give up driving because they cannot see as well as they once could.

The ability to travel freely is basic to participation in volunteer work, social functions, and part-time careers. Older people who turn in their driver's licenses because their vision is not what it used to be may be doing themselves a disservice, the Association says. However, doctors of optometry agree that, while older people generally do not have to give up driving, they should recognize their vision limitations and confine driving activities to places, speeds, and hours when they are most comfortable and competent.

To help older Americans remain active and help them drive safely, the American Optometric Association suggests that older drivers:

—Have a professional vision examination annually to be certain they have the proper vision correction for both day and night driving. (Almost everyone over 45 needs some type of vision correction to compensate for vision changes that occur with age.)

—Wear quality sunglasses during the day to protect the eyes from sunlight glare, but never at night, when they drastically reduce the light needed to see clearly. Due to chemical changes within the eye, older persons need more light to see effectively and are bothered more by glare than younger people.

—Study the cars and roadways far ahead and glance frequently at the rearview mirror and to the sides for signs of danger to compensate for the loss of some peripheral or side vision that occurs with age. This also helps drivers stay alert and anticipate danger.

—Choose a car without a tinted windshield. A tinted windshield reduces the amount of light entering the eyes and can be a handicap at night for the older driver.

—Be sure headlights are clean and adjusted to adequately light the roadway.

—Keep the windshield clean and be sure rearview mirrors are clean and adjusted.

—Because drugs can affect vision, know the side effects of any drugs being taken *before* getting behind the wheel.

—Avoid drinking and smoking, which can both affect the visual skills needed to drive.

Alex Comfort, in his book, *A Good Age,* says that "older, fit drivers are the least dangerous on the road. The two real dangers are poor eyesight and the less obvious one, 'acting out of oldness.'" Older people often learn to walk carefully, for various reasons. "Once in a car," Comfort writes, "these sensibly self-imposed limitations no longer apply, but an older person may then drive the vehicle 'oddly' as if it was the body in question. Their driving becomes a part of their usual non-verbal behavior, expressing lack of confidence in movement." Thus they drive too slowly, indecisively, and often in the middle of the road. Comfort suggests that a few driving lessons will help you become aware that in the car you have a "new, ageless body." He also points out that there are men and women over 80 who still regularly fly airplanes.

Indiana

Donald Finney
Commission on Aging and Aged
Graphic Arts Building
215 N. Senate Avenue
Indianapolis, IN 46202
317-633-5948

Iowa

Odell McGhe
Commission on Aging
415 Tenth Street
Jewett Building
Des Moines, IA 50319
515-281-5187

Kansas

Sheila Reynolds
Kansas Department on Aging
2700 W. 6th Street

Topeka, KS 66606
913-296-4986

Kentucky

Eugene Attkisson
Center for Aging Services
Department for Human Resources
New Human Resources Building
275 E. Main Street
Frankfort, KY 40601
502-564-6930

Louisiana

Ray Dry
Bureau for Aging Services
Office of Human Services
P.O. Box 44282
Capitol Station
Baton Rouge, LA 70804
504-389-2171

Maine

Julie S. Jones
Legal Services for the Elderly
Whitten Road
Augusta, ME 04333
207-289-2561

Maryland

Peter Robb
Office on Aging
State Office Building
301 W. Preston Street
Baltimore, MD 21201
301-383-2100

Massachusetts

J. J. Donovan
Department of Elder Affairs
110 Tremont Street, 5th Floor
Boston, MA 02108
617-727-7273

Michigan

Kathy Coulter
Office of Services to the Aging
3500 N. Logan Street
Lansing, MI 48913
517-373-8560

Minnesota

Betty A. Berger
Governor's Citizens Council on Aging
Metro Square Building, Suite 204
7th and Roberts Streets
St. Paul, MN 55101
612-296-0378

Mississippi

Legal Services Developer
Council on Aging
P.O. Box 5136
Fondren Station
510 George Street
Jackson, MS 39216
601-354-6590

Missouri

Eric Tanner
Law Center for Senior Citizens
1103 Grand Avenue, Suite 310
Kansas City, MO 64106

Montana

Neil Haight
Montana Legal Services
601 Power Block
Helena, MT 59601
406-442-4510

Nebraska

John Vihstadt
Nebraska Commission on Aging
P.O. Box 95044
Lincoln, NE 68509
402-471-2306

Nevada

Chauncey Veatch
Division of Aging Services
Department of Human Resources
505 E. King Street
Kinkead Building, Room 101
Carson City, NV 89710
702-885-4210

New Hampshire

Bill Sitzler
Council on Aging
14 Depot Street
Concord, NH 03301
603-244-3333

New Jersey

Sandy Schussel
Division on Aging
Department of Community Affairs
P.O. Box 2768
363 W. State Street
Trenton, NJ 08625
609-292-8658 or 292-1839

New Mexico

Andres DeAguero
Commission on Aging
408 Galisteo
Villagra Building
Santa Fe, NM 87501
505-827-5258

New York

Robert Bosman
Office for the Aging
New York State Executive Department
Empire State Plaza Building II
Albany, NY 12223
518-474-5796

North Carolina

Robert Hensley
North Carolina Division of Aging
Department of Human Resources
213 Hillsborough Street
Raleigh, NC 27603
919-733-3983

North Dakota

Roger Gette
Legal Assistance of North Dakota, Inc.
420 N. Fourth Street
Bismarck, ND 58501
701-258-4271

Ohio

A. Elizabeth Reuter
Commission on Aging
50 W. Broad Street
Columbus, OH 43215
614-466-6597

Oklahoma

Bill Geyer
Special Unit on Aging
Department of Institutions, Social and
    Rehabilitative Services
P.O. Box 25352
Oklahoma City, OK 73125
405-521-2281

Oregon

Ron Wyden
Oregon Legal Services Corp.
2328 N.W. Everett
Portland, OR 97210
503-223-7502

Pennsylvania

Herbert C. Phillips
Office for the Aging
Department of Public Welfare
P.O. Box 2675
Harrisburg, PA 17120
717-787-1007

Puerto Rico

Elyn Cruz Gomez
Gericulture Commission
Department of Social Services
P.O. Box 11697
Santurce, Puerto Rico 00908
809-722-2429

Rhode Island

Richard Del Sesto
Division on Aging
Department of Elderly Affairs
150 Washington
Providence, RI 02903
401-277-2858

South Carolina

Maxine Coplan
Commission on Aging
915 Main Street
Columbia, SC 29201

South Dakota

Legal Services Developer
Adult Services and Aging
Department of Social Services
State Office Building
Illinois Street
Pierre, SD 57501
605-224-3656

Tennessee

George Franklin
Commission on Aging
S & P Building, Room 102
306 Gay Street
Nashville, TN 37201
615-741-2056

Texas

Doug Richnow
P.O. Box 12786
Capitol Station
Austin, TX 78711
512-475-2863

Utah

Allan Sloan
Division on Aging
Department of Social Services
151 West North Temple
P.O. Box 2500
Salt Lake City, UT 84103
801-533-6422

Vermont

Contact your nearest Area Agency on
Aging.

Virgin Islands

Desmond Maynard
Virgin Islands Commission on Aging
Charlotte Amalie, St. Thomas, Virgin
Islands 00801
809-774-5884
or
Allan Tow
Legal Services of the Virgin Islands
4 Nye Gade
Charlotte Amalie, St. Thomas, Virgin
Islands 00801
809-774-6720

Virginia

Gloria Cordes-Macklin
Legal Service Corporation of Virginia
700 E. Main Street, Room 1428
Richmond, VA 23219
804-782-9438

Washington

Gregory Potegal
Office on Aging
Department of Social and Health
Services
Mail Stop OB 43G
Olympia, WA 98504
206-753-2502

West Virginia

Alice Loeb
West Virginia Commission on Aging
State Capitol
Charleston, WV 25305
304-348-2241

Wisconsin

Maxine Austin
Division of Community Services
Department of Health and Social
Services
110 E. Main, Room 202
Madison, WI 53702
608-266-2536

Wyoming

Steve Vajda
Division of Public Assistance
Office on Aging
Hathaway Building
Cheyenne, WY 82002
307-777-7561

Elderworks

For many years, the Edna McConnell Clark Foundation was the leading private philanthropy in the field of aging. Unlike most government programs, which tend to view older people essentially as needy consumers of service, the Clark Foundation's grants were based on the notion that older people represent an underutilized resource for the public good. Most of its funds were allocated to create job opportunities in programs where the energies of able older people could be directed to solving social and economic problems in their own communities—in school districts, in colleges and universities, in hospital outreach services, in home care, and in legal services.

Although the Clark Foundation no longer funds programs on aging, a new public foundation has been formed, starting in 1979, for the specific purpose of helping institutions recruit and make better use of older people in both paid and volunteer jobs. Elderworks, whose president, Merrell M. Clark, was formerly with the Clark Foundation, will solicit funds from the public to support its work. For information, write:

Elderworks
Merrell M. Clark
680 Fifth Avenue
New York, NY 10019

Tax-Aides

The income tax laws that affect older people, including the very ones designed to save them money, are so complicated and ever-changing that many of these taxpayers end up paying more than they should, or not receiving the rebates to which they are entitled. United States tax authorities estimate that half of the nine million older Americans who file federal returns pay more than they are required to. Others, not actually required to file returns, lose out on rebates that they would have received if they had filed.

To meet this problem, the National Retired Teachers Association/National Association of Retired Persons (NRTA/AARP) has instituted a large-scale Tax-Aide program. Last year alone, more than 7500 volunteers helped well over half a million low-income and elderly

The AARP Tax-Aide program provides trained volunteer counselors to assist other older people in completing their income tax returns. In 1978, 7500 volunteers helped more than 600,000 individuals file their returns. *Photo credit: AARP*

people file their income taxes. The goal of the Tax-Aide program is to reach a million people by 1980.

You don't have to be a member of NRTA/AARP to volunteer your services. Anyone with experience in filling out his or her tax forms is welcome. If you have tax or accounting experience, you will be pressed into service as an instructor, as well as a tax counselor. Training sessions last from one to five days and are given in cooperation with the Internal Revenue Service. The Tax-Aide program runs from February 1 to April 15 and volunteers must work a minimum of four hours a week.

Although Tax-Aides work primarily in walk-in centers, many areas send volunteers to homebound people as well as those in nursing homes or other institutions. In rural areas, in the West particularly, teams go out to remote communities once or twice each tax season.

A common problem the volunteers see is that of the newly widowed person who has never before taken care of his or her own income taxes.

(Although this is more likely to be a woman, it isn't always.) So-called tax credits for the elderly are another source of confusion. Many people assume this to mean all elderly, whereas it actually is designed for retired civil servants who do not get social security payments. A very real tax break for low-income people over 65 has to do with selling a home, since they don't have to pay a capital gains tax on a sale under $35,000.

If you would like more information about the Tax-Aide program and an application to become a volunteer, write:

NRTA/AARP Tax-Aide Program
1909 K Street, N.W.
Washington, DC 20049

SCORE (Service Corps of Retired Executives)

If providing legal and tax services are the newest areas of high-level volunteering opportunities for older people, SCORE is one of the oldest. Since 1964, retired business executives have responded to almost half a million requests for assistance. Today, there are 6000 SCORE volunteers working out of nearly 300 chapters in all fifty states and Puerto Rico.

SCORE is sponsored by the Small Business Administration (SBA), which offers both small-business loans and management assistance. SCORE volunteers staff the regional SBA offices and do on-site counseling in every facet of business management. The volunteers come from all fields; they are former retailers, production analysts, office managers, lawyers, bankers, engineers, accountants, economists, government employees, advertising and public relations experts, and owners and managers of small businesses of every description. Their former affiliations sometimes read like a roster of the *Fortune* 500.

The need for volunteers varies from area to area, although local chapters are always looking for people to fill gaps in expertise. Some SCORE members, like an 80-year-old former owner of a clothing store in New Bedford, Massachusetts, find themselves working almost full time.

SCORE is a very local operation. Look it up under the Small Business Administration in the U.S. Government section of the telephone book, or write:

SCORE
Small Business Administration
1441 L Street, N.W.
Washington, DC 20416

President Jimmy Carter greets his old advisor, Tom Perry, a SCORE volunteer from Atlanta. "When I went home from the Navy, I didn't have any money and I didn't have any business training. After starting my own family business ... I went to the Small Business Administration. They gave me a loan and they assigned me a very distinguished retired businessman from Atlanta to advise me. The guidance and assistance that SCORE gave me made all the difference between success and failure."

ACE (Active Corps of Executives)

ACE was established about ten years ago as a supplement to SCORE. The only difference is that the 2600 ACE volunteers are still active in the business world.

For further information, see SCORE, above.

International Executive Service Corps

This private, nonprofit organization recruits experienced executives, usually retired, from U.S. firms to serve in the developing countries as volunteer advisors to locally owned enterprises that request managerial or technical assistance. The assignments average two or three months and travel and living expenses for the volunteers and their spouses are supplied. There is no salary.

Since it began operating in 1965, more than 6000 volunteers have completed assignments in sixty-three countries in Latin America, Asia, the Middle East, Africa, and eastern Europe. The majority of the requests come from private enterprises. Serving these clients, volunteer executives have helped solve problems in the production of food and clothing, manufacturing operations of many kinds and sizes, construction in all fields, transportation, communications, banking and finance, marketing, and the media. Each executive assigned to a project works with a designated counterpart in the client organization.

For information about current recruiting needs, write or call:
Vice President—Executive Recruitment
International Executive Service Corps
622 Third Avenue
New York, NY 10017
212-490-6800

Executive Volunteer Corps

This is a New York City group associated with the city's Economic Development Administration. A staff of retired businessmen is made up of specialists in a large variety of fields. If you wish to volunteer your expertise, write or call:
Executive Volunteer Corps
Economic Development Administration
415 Madison Avenue
New York, NY 10017
212-593-8964

Senior Interns

Under a relatively new but growing Congressional Senior Intern program, older people active in elder affairs in their own communities spend a week or two in May in the Washington offices of their senators and representatives. In 1978, more than 150 people took part; seventy House and Senate offices acted as sponsors. The program is designed to familiarize the interns with legislation and other governmental activities in the area of aging — and, in reverse, to familiarize Washington with the views of those at home who are knowledgeable in the field.

The interns spend about half of their time working for their representatives or senators in their offices; the pay helps defray the cost of the trip. Congressmen select their own interns, often from established organizations in their districts. Clearly, with a program as small as this one, there are a great many more applicants than can be accepted.

For information, write your representative or senator.

Society of Retired Executives

Nonprofit organizations, city and state agencies, small businesses, and high schools and colleges have benefited from the advice, consultation, and research activities of this organization, which is sponsored by the Indianapolis Chamber of Commerce. About 250 members have been involved in more than 300 projects, including management studies for the city, career counseling, and supplementing the teaching of courses in economics and business. The Retired Professors of Indiana recently became affiliated with the Society.

For information, write or call:
Society of Retired Executives
320 North Meridian Street
Indianapolis, IN 46204
317-635-4747

SMC (Senior Medical Consultants)

SMC is an organization formed for the teaching of medicine, offering one of the most distinguished physician rosters in medical education. There are more than 120 physician consultants in SMC.

The purpose of SMC is to bring quality teaching programs to the

Helen Cope, an 88-year-old retired social worker from Farmington, Michigan, with Senator Robert P. Griffin. Mrs. Cope took part in the 1978 Congressional Senior Intern program.

many community hospitals that are not affiliated with medical schools and are not large enough to offer full-scale teaching programs for their medical staffs by their own staff physicians.

The physicians who join SMC have all been active clinicians or practitioners throughout their careers, which have included teaching posts at leading medical schools in the New York City area. They are also motivated by a desire to continue teaching, to contribute to medical education, even though most have been subject to mandatory retirement at their own teaching institutions.

SMC is an AMA-accredited organization in Continuing Medical Education. Its long-range goal is to become a national program.

For information, write:

Senior Medical Consultants
30 East 60th Street
New York, NY 10022

Literacy Volunteers of America has chapters in thirteen states. Recruits take an intensive training course before meeting with their students. *Photo credit: Frank Shoemaker*

Law Enforcement

The Crime, Safety, and the Senior Citizen Program of the International Association of Chiefs of Police has, as one of its goals, the use of older people as volunteers in local law enforcement agencies. For information, see pages 89–90.

Literacy Volunteers of America

This private, nonprofit agency recruits people of all age groups to tutor people in basic reading and English as a second language. Literacy Volunteers of America currently has eighty local chapters tutoring more than 10,000 persons. Volunteers are prepared for the work through an eighteen-hour basic reading workshop or a fifteen-hour English as a Second Language workshop. Persons interested in becoming volunteers or establishing chapters are asked to write or call:

Literacy Volunteers of America, Inc.
700 E. Water Street
Syracuse, NY 13201
315-474-7039

CHAPTER 6

Community Programs for Older People—A Guide to Setting Up Local Projects

Programs for older people are proliferating with such speed and in such variety that there is almost no way to keep track of them. This chapter, designed to help people and organizations start projects in local communities, does not pretend to cover the many possibilities—in fact, the author would appreciate hearing about programs that should be included in a future book of this sort. What you will find here are guidelines on how to go about starting an older-persons activity, some examples of things others have done to meet a variety of needs, and addresses of places and people that can help your organization get started.

Funding Sources

Finding appropriate funding sources for projects and programs relating to aging can be an overwhelming task, but A *National Guide to Government and Foundation Funding Sources in the Field of Aging* makes the job much easier. The guide lists information on public and private funding and federal assistance, with information on federal restrictions, uses, eligibility, and application procedures.

Data is provided on more than eighty-five federal funding programs in such categories as funding under the Older Americans Act, employment, volunteerism, economic self-sufficiency, community development, and housing and construction.

Other categories include physical and mental health, nutrition, transportation, education and training, the arts and humanities, social and behavioral research, and supportive and protective services.

The price of the guide is $13.50. It is available from:

Adelphi University Press
Levermore Hall 103
Garden City, NY 11530

Finding the Facts

Basic to any service is solid information about the people to be served. There is no dearth of facts about the older population in America—on the contrary, there is so much raw data that anyone looking for information can easily be swamped with material, as the author has found out. In recognition of this need, and as a contribution to professionals who provide services to the elderly, the National Council on the Aging published, in 1978, the *Fact Book on Aging: A Profile of America's Older Population.* The *Fact Book,* designed as a convenient reference volume for program planners, consolidates information from a wide variety of sources, and categorizes, summarizes, and describes the current state of knowledge about the older population. It is more than worth its cost. For a copy, send $10 to:

The National Council on the Aging, Inc.
1828 L Street, N.W.
Washington, DC 20036

Older Volunteers

Although many successful programs exist only because of the services of older volunteers, many more community projects could make use of this too-often untapped source of volunteer expertise. A useful booklet for program planners is *Realizing the Potential of the Older Volunteer,* published by the Ethel Percy Andrus Gerontology Center. A project of the Older Volunteer Program (see page 49), the monograph describes the experiences, satisfactions, and frustrations of the senior volunteers who pioneered in the Andrus Center. It is a useful guide for locating the natural leadership talents that are widespread among retired adults and for finding meaningful ways to use their knowledge and experience in a variety of organizational settings within the community.

For a copy of the booklet, send $3.50 to:
Publications Office
Andrus Gerontology Center
University of Southern California
Los Angeles, CA 90007

Films on Aging

About Aging: A Catalogue of Films lists more than 300 films that concern the many facets of aging. The book, published by the Ethel Percy Andrus Gerontology Center, gives a description of each film, where it can be rented or purchased, and how much it costs.

The catalogue has become a standard reference throughout the U.S. and in many other countries.

A selection of feature-length and foreign films has been added and more than 300 films are described that cover thirty-four separate categories of interest. Among them are problems, realities, and some solutions of aging, community services, crime and consumer protection, death and dying, employment, health maintenance, home care, housing, income, mental health, nursing, recreation and leisure, rural and urban aged, sexuality, and welfare.

The book may be obtained for $3.50 plus 35¢ postage and handling charge from:
Publications Office
Andrus Gerontology Center
University of Southern California
University Park
Los Angeles, CA 90007

Women and Aging

There are many more older women than there are older men and, ironically, although they live longer than men, women are beset by the problems of growing old at a much earlier age and in many more ways—what Susan Sontag has called the double standard of aging. Although aging is a different experience for women, information about the status of the older woman isn't easy to find.

"Look through any bibliography on aging and you will discover that older women are practically non-existent," writes Tish Sommer, coordinator of the NOW Older Women's Rights Committee (formerly the

Task Force on Older Women). "At 65 we not only are presumed to lose our sexuality but even our gender. We suddenly join a new category — senior citizens or the aged — with little attention to the differences of aging between the sexes in our society."

To answer a constant bombardment of requests from women's studies programs, librarians, students of gerontology, and older women themselves, the NOW group arranged to have such a bibliography compiled. *Age Is Becoming: An Annotated Bibliography on Women and Aging* covers selected material published between 1970 and 1977.

For a copy, send $3 to:
Interface Bibliographers
3018 Hillegass Avenue
Berkeley, CA 94705

Information and Referral Directories

When Harry H. Henry, a retired civil-service worker from Oakland, California, visited friends in a large retirement community, he came away impressed by the number of activities and services he found there. Wondering why his own city couldn't provide similar resources for older people, he went to the mayor of Oakland to discuss the subject. As he related what he had found in the retirement community, the mayor told him, "We have these things, too."

The problem was that few people knew about them. Cheerfully giving up his post-retirement "freedom," Henry set about remedying the information gap. His sixty-five-page *Directory of Services for Senior Citizens* covers virtually every subject of concern to older people, "whatever is important to survival, pleasure, and economy." Some of the more popular sections pertain to merchants offering discounts; health organizations that provide low-cost services; legal assistance; transportation savings; low-cost hot meals; rental facilities where the elderly are preferred; adult education; recreation; and information on tax exemptions. Other listings include retirement housing facilities, part-time job agencies, home health care, and housekeepers and drivers at reasonable rates. Henry's directory for the San Francisco Bay area is updated every six months and has been placed in the libraries in most of the cities in the region.

To help individuals and organizations in other parts of the country set up their own local directories, Henry has produced a thirty-five-page do-it-yourself kit. It is available free, from:
Harry H. Henry
P.O. Box 1822
Oakland, CA 94612

Newsletters and Newspapers

Most of the dozens of newsletters I've read in the course of researching this book are the official publications of state or city offices on aging or of the membership organizations of older people. In quality they range from bad to pretty good, but the emphasis in the contents is always heavily on the activities sponsored by the parent publisher. One brilliant exception is a bimonthly, sixteen-page newspaper, *Senior Summary,* published by the New York Junior League.

Conceived in 1974 as a way of informing the elderly people of Yorkville, a New York City neighborhood, of the services available to them, the paper has grown steadily until it now has a 35,000-copy print run and covers a large part of Manhattan with news and feature stories as well as descriptions of community resources. The illustrated tabloid-sized newspaper is well written, lively and informative, and extremely well produced.

Senior Summary is distributed free through neighborhood senior centers, churches, banks, libraries, supermarkets, apartment buildings, museums, thrift shops, and the telephone company offices. Single copies are mailed only to persons who cannot pick up a copy themselves or who live outside of Manhattan, but the increasing number of requests for these is becoming a financial problem.

In its December 1977 issue, *Senior Summary* describes its own birth and growth, the obstacles it met and how they were surmounted, as well as the problems it sees in the future, most of them the by-product of its escalating success. Any organization looking for guidelines on how to start a newsletter will find this a useful text. Those that already publish one might look at any issue to see how well it can be done.

For information, write:
Senior Summary
New York Junior League
130 E. 80th Street
New York, NY 10021

USE (Useful Services Exchange)

If you are good at carpentry and I like gardening, why should each of us pay money we cannot afford to have someone else do for us what we could do for each other? This is the basic premise behind the many service exchanges that are popping up in communities all over the country. Some are designed specifically for older people and some are not; the principle is still the same.

In Reston, Virginia, Useful Services Exchange (USE) was started by Henry Ware, an economist with experience in marketing and bartering systems. USE has about 500 members, who exchange services on an hourly basis. If, for example, a member spends two hours repairing your television set, then you owe him or her two hours of some other kind of work. Glenn Ellison, the oldest participating member, repairs lamps and household appliances and helps neighbors with picture framing. Prudence Herrick, 79, is an artist who works regularly at the art gallery. In exchange for designing recipe cards with gourmet illustrations, letterheads, and posters, she receives free transportation by various other members.

As a result of much publicity, USE has been flooded with requests for information on how to set up similar exchanges. To provide a clearing-house of information and experience, the Association of USE, Inc., has been formed.

For information, write, enclosing a stamped, self-addressed envelope, to:

USE
Wellborn Building
1614 Washington Plaza
Reston, VA 22090

Anticrime Programs

There are several national projects related to crime and the elderly. The Administration on Aging, in conjunction with the Law Enforcement Assistance Administration, the Community Services Administration, and the Department of Housing and Urban Development, is sponsoring demonstration projects designed to reduce the impact of crime against the elderly in six cities—New York, Los Angeles, Washington, Milwaukee, New Orleans, and Chicago. The cities were selected primarily on the basis of demographic and geographic characteristics that will enhance efforts to generalize the results to the widest possible number of cities.

Other anticrime programs are underway in other cities, including Kansas City, Missouri, and Muskogee, Oklahoma.

In every state, the State Criminal Justice Planning Agency receives federal grants to design and implement programs to reduce crime against older people. Write or call your State Office on Aging (see appendix) for the address and telephone number of the Criminal Justice Planning Agency in your state.

In Rochester, New York, under a state-funded pilot program, Neighborhood Radio Watch, police have installed citizens band radios in a hundred homes. Police cars in the area monitor channel nine, the national emergency channel, for calls from the participants. The CBs serve a double purpose, since those who have them can use the twenty-two other channels to talk to friends.

The International Association of Chiefs of Police, under a grant from the Administration on Aging, is currently involved in a project on Crime, Safety, and the Senior Citizen. The goals of this project are the development of crime prevention programs and the utilization of older volunteers in local law enforcement agencies. In addition, the Association has produced a national directory of crime prevention programs for senior citizens. To get a copy, write:

International Association of Chiefs of Police
11 Firstfield Road
Gaithersburg, MD 20760

The American Association of Retired Persons (AARP), under a grant from the Law Enforcement Assistance Administration, has developed a 574-page training manual, *Law Enforcement and Older Persons,* for use at any level of police training. The grant and the manual stemmed from the more than 130 seminars the AARP has conducted for law enforcement personnel since 1973. The AARP also publishes a free thirty-page anticrime guide for individuals. For information about the police training program, write:

American Association of Retired Persons
1909 K Street, N.W.
Washington, DC 20049

For a copy of the *Retirement Anti-Crime Guide,* write:

Anti-Crime Guide
AARP
P.O. Box 2240
Long Beach, CA 90801

Physical Health and Psychological Counseling

Guidelines for an Information and Counseling Service for Older Persons offers guidance in establishing and implementing a program of physical health and psychological counseling. The guide costs $2.00 and is available from:

Information and Counseling Service for Older Persons
Box 2914
Duke University Medical Center
Durham, NC 27706

MAP (Mutual Aid Project)

MAP is a new program sponsored by the Citizens Committee for New York City, Inc., and supported by a number of grants, to help older people in neighborhoods provide services for themselves. MAP is a salaried, ten-member resource and organizing group. The organizers function as advice-givers and providers of technical support to groups and individuals requesting assistance—in all cases, it is up to the people in the neighborhoods, not the organizers, to decide what projects are needed or desired. The organizers begin by working with such existing organizations as block and tenant associations, senior centers, and religious and social clubs. At present the organizers are working in four areas in Brooklyn and the Bronx.

MAP publishes newsletters, in both English and Spanish, that describe the kind of self-help activities now going on throughout New York. It also prepares and distributes handbooks and other materials regarding specific project ideas and issues arising from its work. The first of these to be published is a handsome, illustrated (and paid for by private funds) book, *The Older Person's Handbook: Ideas, Projects, and Resources for Neighborhood Action.* Among the subjects covered are self-protection projects, projects for the homebound, consumer education projects, cooperative and exchange projects, and urban gardening.

Although the book is specific to New York City, it is an excellent guide for any group in any city or town that is interested in setting up mutual aid projects for older people. For a copy, write or call:

MAP Central Office
17 Murray Street
New York, NY 10007
212-349-8155

Senior Tutors

In Redding, Connecticut, a project that brings senior tutors together with learning-troubled adolescents has proved so successful that the school district has prepared a manual to help others who might want to set up similar programs. Although S.T.E.P.—Senior Tutors for Educational Progress—is "a model of simplicity in design and implementation," the program, according to Superintendent of Schools Lawrence R. Miller, has its own intricacies. The comprehensive manual appraises these frankly and offers specific help in setting up a S.T.E.P. program, from selecting a program director to advertising for tutors (in Redding they are paid $2.50 an hour and work fifteen hours a week), to training, evaluation, working with parents, and all of the other things that go into making a successful program. For a copy of the manual, write:

Mrs. Rosalie Saul
Project S.T.E.P.
Redding Elementary School
Redding, CT 06875

Senior Employment Services

A new association has been formed to help independent senior employment agencies improve their services. It will also serve as a source of guidance for individuals and organizations interested in starting such an agency in their own communities. For information, write:

Thomas Bradley
Association of Employment Services for the Elderly
National Council on the Aging
1828 L Street
Washington, DC 20036

Theater Groups

Although a number of local organizations, like Articulture in Cambridge, Massachusetts, are beginning to provide entertainment and performers for senior centers and nursing homes, an even newer type of program is the theater group. Original plays that celebrate old age, performed by acting troupes of older people, are an exciting (one is tempted to say dramatic) innovation.

TOP (Theatre for Older People) is a project of the Joseph Jefferson Theatre Company, a professional off-off-Broadway group. The resident company is made up of older Actor's Equity performers and the administrative director who thought up the idea, is Susan Miller, gerontologist with a theater background. TOP uses the theater as both an educational and entertainment medium. Its original one-act plays dramatize issues that are crucial to older people and the performances are followed by discussions led by professionals in the teaching and mental health fields. TOP also offers to conduct workshops in drama, writing, sexuality, and intergenerational relations, also led by professionals in those areas.

TOP performs at its own quarters, the Little Church Around the Corner, and on tour before groups throughout New York City and Westchester, Long Island, and New Jersey.

Prime Time, a play about older people, is performed by three members of TOP, Theatre for Older People, a project of the Joseph Jefferson Theatre Company in New York.

The cost to an organization for a play and discussion ranges from $150 to $300, depending on the play. The fee for a workshop is $75.

For information, write or call:

Connie Alexis

TOP (Theatre for Older People)

Joseph Jefferson Theatre Company, Inc.

1 E. 29th Street

New York, NY 10016

212-679-7174

As the Second City, Chicago has in the past been famous for its innovative theater groups, and the Chicago Free Street Theater Group is following in that tradition. All of the performers in Chicago Free Street

Too are at least 65 years old, but they aren't professional actors who have refused to retire. Recruited through a newspaper advertisement, they include a former librarian, bank clerk, engineer, teacher, pianist, and professor. The seven-person cast has performed at home and across the country before 25,000 people and has begun to tour with the parent company.

Other theater groups are following Chicago Free Street Too's example. In Louisville, Kentucky, the Actors Theater has a Senior Players group. Back Alley Theater in Washington has SAGE (Society for Artistic Growth of the Elderly). In Skokie, Illinois, the Oakton Community College has Acting Up. A group in Cincinnati has been started by the Area Senior Services; one in Columbia, Missouri, by the National Benevolent Association of the United Church of Christ.

For guidance in starting a theater group, write:

The Center on Arts and the Aging

The National Council on the Aging

1828 L Street, N.W.

Washington, DC 20036

Humanistic Gerontology

Sometimes described as "this crazy group in Berkeley that's turning old people on," SAGE (Senior Actualization and Growth Experiences) is a "humanistically focused self-development program" for men and women over 60. The staff and clientele of SAGE have been exploring some of the many ways in which the later years of life can be a time for "health, vitality, expanded awareness, and the realization of self that comes from having lived a long and full life."

When SAGE began in 1974, the project knew of few people who were attempting to incorporate personal growth and holistic health methods and beliefs in their work with older people. However, through its outreach and training programs, SAGE became aware that there are "thousands" of people and institutions actively involved in trying to facilitate positive and creative images of aging and services to the aged. Although there has been a growing body of information that supports a humanistic approach to gerontology, there has been no organization to act as a clearing-house and central resource for all of the ideas, techniques, materials, experiences, and programs.

In response to this need, SAGE has spawned the National Association for Humanistic Gerontology. Its specific purpose is to create a national network of people, institutions, and programs related to the humanistic approach to aging. Membership is open to anyone, professionals and nonprofessionals alike.

For information, write:
SAGE-NAHG
Claremont Office Park
41 Tunnel Road
Berkeley, CA 94705

Senior Center Humanities Program

With funds from the National Endowment for the Humanities, a new program in the humanities is available to senior centers. Sponsored by the National Council on Aging (NCOA), the program offers units on

Members of SAGE (Senior Actualization and Growth Experiences) on a hike near Berkeley, California. SAGE is a humanistically focused self-development program for men and women over 60. The group has been exploring some of the ways in which the later years of life can be a time for health, vitality, and expanded awareness.
Photo credit: Karen R. Preuss

such topics as the American Family, Exploring Local History (an eight-week unit), and Images of Aging in Literature.

For information, write:

Ronald Alvarez, Director
Senior Center Humanities Program
National Council on the Aging
1828 L Street, N.W.
Washington, DC 20036

Foster Grandparent Program

For a description of the program, see chapter 5.

Any public or nonprofit private agency or organization may apply for a grant from ACTION, which pays up to 90 percent of the total cost of development and operation of the projects. Many state legislatures, however, have appropriated additional funds, as have sponsoring agencies and other community organizations.

For information, call your regional ACTION office (listed under U.S. Government) or write or call, toll-free:

ACTION
806 Connecticut Avenue, N.W.
Washington, DC 20525
800-424-8580

Senior Companions

For a description, see chapter 5.

Guidelines are similar to those for the Foster Grandparent Program, although the program is much newer and smaller.

For information, see ACTION, above.

RSVP (Retired Senior Volunteer Program)

For a description of the program, see chapter 5.

Any established community organization may request the services of a Retired Senior Volunteer. Typical volunteer stations include courts, schools, libraries, day-care centers, hospitals, nursing homes, economic development agencies, and other community service centers. For information, see ACTION, above.

A Foster Grandparent gives a smile and a hug to a child at the Corpus Christi State School in Texas.

Exercise Programs

Exercise programs for older people are springing up in centers and communities all over the country. Much help is available for any group that wants to set up a program.

Training materials and promotional posters and flyers ("Join the Active People Over 60"), as well as slides, films, and an audio-visual "mini workshop" are available at cost from:

National Association for Human Development
1750 Pennsylvania Avenue, N.W.
Washington, DC 20006

A booklet, *Exercises for the Elderly,* based on an exercise show produced for the University of Iowa Educational Broadcasting Network, is available for 65¢ a copy from:

Dr. David K. Leslie
Field House, Room 205
University of Iowa
Iowa City, IA 52242

A personal exercise regimen based on the one developed by the President's Council on Physical Fitness appears in chapter 8. The executive director of the council is actively involved in setting up exercise programs throughout the country. For information, write:

C. Carson Conrad, Executive Director

President's Council on Physical Fitness

Department of Health, Education and Welfare

Washington, DC 20201

The Institute for Creative Aging in California has developed an unusual holistic approach to developing body and mind. Its format involves a "select group of teachings and exercises culled from Western therapeutic methods and Eastern philosophies in a balanced program designed for self-improvement and growth." The Institute believes its program can be adapted and used by institutions and community groups throughout the country.

The program includes classes in acupressure, biofeedback, counseling, deep breathing, Feldenkrais exercises, guided imagery, Hatha yoga, massage, meditation, music and art therapy, and Tai Chi Chuan.

For information, wirte:

Institute for Creative Aging

11730 Sunset Boulevard

Los Angeles, CA 90049

CHAPTER 7

Work: Jobs and Employment Agencies

For economic and psychological reasons, almost one third of the people who retire return to the job market. Social security officials report that not only are more retired people than ever going back to work, but that their overall income from working equals that of their income from social security. Today, half a million "retired" workers earn more than $3000 a year, which until recently was the limit before social security payments were reduced.

Under the new law, people over 72 are exempt from any limitation on earnings in order to receive their social security payments. In 1982, the age at which there will be no forfeiture will be dropped to 70. Meanwhile, in 1979 the limit on outside earnings is $4500; in 1980 it will be $5000, and in 1981, $5500.

Clearly, retirement means a new life for some people and death for others. Literally, according to Representative Claude Pepper who at 77 was a leader in the fight to raise the mandatory retirement age from 65 to 70. According to Pepper, mortality rates for people who were *forced* to retire were 30 percent higher than normal for the same age group. Dr. Robert N. Butler, Director of the National Institute on Aging, agrees that there are serious physiological effects when a person whose whole identity was tied up in doing something substantial (in this case, work) loses that sense of purpose. Pointing out that self-employed people who like their work don't retire if they can help it, he agrees that for some people the retirement syndrome can be devastating.

The American Medical Association agrees. In a policy statement opposing arbitrary retirement based on chronological age, its Committee on Aging has stated that "arbitrary retirement and denial of work opportunity—whether the work is for pay or the pleasure of giving—seriously threatens the health of the individual concerned." It adds that "there is ample clinical evidence that physical and emotional problems can be precipitated or exacerbated by denial of employment opportunities."

On January 1, 1979, the age at which an employee may be forced to retire was raised from 65 to 70. The new law is an amendment to the Age Discrimination in Employment Act (ADEA). It now prohibits employment discrimination against individuals between the ages of 40 and 70. It does not require persons to work until they are 70 nor does it change the age eligibility for collecting social security or other retirement benefits.

The law affects most people in private employment and most state

Representative Claude Pepper of Florida, who led the fight to raise the mandatory retirement age from 65 to 70, is interviewed outside the Capitol. The man to his right is an interpreter for the deaf. Far right, William Hutton, president of the National Council of Senior Citizens.

and local government employees. There are certain exceptions: the law does not apply to employees of a firm with twenty or fewer workers; it does not affect tenured college professors unless they are covered by a state law—this exemption will expire in 1982—and certain executives may be retired if their retirement benefits total $27,000 a year, exclusive of social security.

The new law also banishes mandatory retirement at any age for most federal employees. Exemptions include law-enforcement officers, CIA officials, air-traffic controllers, and fire fighters.

If you have questions concerning your rights under the new law, write:

Age Discrimination Project
American Association of Retired Persons
1909 K Street, N.W.
Washington, DC 20049

Age Discrimination in the Programs on Aging

The next time you check in on your state, city, area, or other agency on aging, find out the ages of the people *they* employ. "A final example of unconscious ageism in government is the inevitable take-over by younger persons of anything related to aging with dollars attached," says Tish Sommers, Coordinator of NOW's Older Women's Rights Committee. Testifying before the House Select Committee on Aging, she described examples of "the invisible, ubiquitous, and largely unexplored ageism in government programs." In California, Sommers said, the Department on Aging employs seventy-seven full-time persons, of whom only four are over 60, "despite the intent of the Older Americans Act to give preference in employment to the age group served."

Low-Income Employment Opportunities

The basic federally supported program for low-income workers over the age of 55 is known as the Senior Community Services Employment Program. It is administered by the U.S. Department of Labor and funded under Title IX of the Older Americans Act. All told, it provides full- or part-time jobs to about 47,000 low-income people—or about 1 percent of the nearly 5 million who would be eligible by age and income to participate.

Five national contractors administer the SCSEP with funds from the Department of Labor. Although the names of the individual programs may be different, all have the same age and income requirements and the same goals: to employ older workers in needed community services.

For information about the available jobs in your area, call or write to the national offices of the sponsoring agencies, which are given below.

Green Thumb
This is a program for rural areas and small cities and towns. Sponsored by the National Farmers Union, Green Thumb, Inc., employs 13,000 people in forty states. As the name implies, the original emphasis of the program was on highway beautification and development. Even in its early days in the late Sixties, however, Green Thumb workers provided services to the rural elderly poor, through home repair, transportation, and nutrition services. Today about half of the Green Thumb jobs are in direct service to the elderly.

For information, write or call:
Green Thumb, Inc.
National Farmers Union
1012 14th Street, N.W.
Washington, DC 20005
202-638-2769

Forest Service Senior Community Service Employment Program
The U.S. Forest Service employs 2500 people in work on national forest lands in thirty-nine states and Puerto Rico. Participants work an average of twenty-four hours a week in conservation and improvement of the forest resources. Like Green Thumb, the program is for people in rural areas. Look up Forest Service under U.S. Government in the telephone directory.

AARP Senior Community Service Employment Program
The aim of the AARP project, typical of all of the SCSEP programs, is to provide on-the-job training to low-income people with the goal of having them eventually find employment in nonsubsidized work. About 8000 people are employed in this project in ninety sites. Most are placed in environmental programs—noise control, water quality, etc.—and with public service agencies.

For information, write or call:
Senior Community Service Employment Program
American Association of Retired Persons
1909 K Street, N.W.
Washington, DC 20049
202-872-4700

Senior Aides

Sponsored by the National Council of Senior Citizens, approximately 7000 Senior Aides work in community services of all kinds in 118 areas all over the country. Work assignments are generally limited to twenty hours a week and are extremely varied, depending on the needs of the local agency requesting the aide.

For information, write or call:
Senior Aides
National Council of Senior Citizens
1511 K Street, N.W.
Washington, DC 20005
202-347-8800

Senior Community Service Project

The National Council on the Aging administers this program, which provides on-the-job training and work experience in thirty communities. Participants are assigned to positions with public and private non-profit agencies. Some of the projects are: paralegal aides, home repair, juvenile detention center, bilingual teachers' aides, employment aides, nutrition aides, and homemaker assistance for the elderly.

For information, write:
Senior Community Service Project
The National Council on the Aging, Inc.
1828 L Street, N.W.
Washington, DC 20036

Employment Agencies

The job market for older people is anything but wide open, particularly for those who want work that matches their skills and experience. Going to a regular employment agency, whether state or private, can be a traumatic as well as futile experience. Your chances are better, particu-

CETA — Not for Older People

Although government agencies that answered my requests for information about employment opportunities for low-income older people usually included CETA as a resource, CETA programs are not included in this book. For a good reason. CETA (Comprehensive Employment and Training Act) is the country's major manpower program, funded in the billions of dollars annually. But CETA emphasizes preparation for work, which in most states excludes all but the young.

CETA officials counter with the argument that people over 55 have their own Senior Community Services Employment programs, described in this chapter. This minuscule program can fund jobs for about 1 percent of the people eligible by age and income. As Tish Sommers says, a crust of bread is better than nothing, but let's not call it a whole loaf. The Senior Community Service jobs, what few there are, pay about $2.70 an hour for a twenty-hour week, or $226 a month. CETA employees work a forty-hour week and earn up to $833 a month.

Nor is there any validity to the argument that the senior jobs are supplemented by social security payment, since the program is open to people at 55, long before they are eligible for social security.

larly in the part-time work field, at one of the agencies specifically for older workers listed in this chapter. None of them charges a fee to the job-seeker and all of them, except for Mature Temps, are nonprofit services. While every attempt was made to find all of the older worker employment services in the country, it is certain that some have been missed. So if you don't find an agency listed for your area, you can find out if there is one by calling your local Area Office on Aging. Look it up in the telephone book under U.S. Government. Or write your state Office on Aging, listed in the back of this book, which should have that information too.

A number of cities have Forty-Plus Clubs. These are executive placement organizations, but since those that replied to our questionnaire indicated that the people served were 40 plus not very much, these agencies are not listed here. The jobs are mostly full-time or as a consultant.

Mature Temps

This company, with offices in twelve cities, claims there are more good jobs than there are good people to fill them. Although not specifically an employment agency for older workers, Joan Fallon, of the Boston office, says they especially like retired people "because they have so much experience and are so dependable." Fallon says they place "lots of people in their seventies." If you have good typing, clerical, secretarial, or other office skills, and live in or near a city where the company has an office, this is a good bet for part-time work. There is no fee and you can work as little or as much as you like.

Mature Temps is recommended by the American Association of Retired Persons (AARP). It is, not coincidentally, a member of the Colonial Penn Group, which also includes the insurance companies that write health, homeowners, and life insurance for AARP members. Nevertheless, the AARP endorsement should mean that no qualified applicant will be denied a job on the basis of age.

Mature Temps has offices in Baltimore; Boston; Chicago; Dallas; Houston; Los Angeles; New York; Philadelphia; Plymouth Meeting, Pennsylvania; San Francisco; White Plains, New York; and Washington, D.C. Check the white pages of your telephone directory or write or call:

Mature Temps
1114 Avenue of the Americas
New York, NY 10036
212-730-7020

Arizona

Second Forty Survival, Inc.

1672 North Magnolia Avenue
Tucson, AZ 85712
602-326-6739

Second Forty Survival is a "caring self-help organization where women take practical, preventative steps to ease the problems of growing older in a sexist, ageist so-

ciety." Job development, counseling, and placement are part of the program.

California

Jobs for Older Women Action Project

3102 Telegraph Avenue
Berkeley, CA 94705
415-849-0332

Jobs for Older Women is a "self-help advocacy group whose purpose is to effect changes that increase self-esteem, independence, and employment opportunities for women." Although it is *not* an employment agency, it does have contact with most of the job-market resources in the area and is provided with current job listings from those sources. It conducts a weekly self-help job meeting, helps women update their skills, and has the help of the California Rural Legal Assistance-Senior Citizen Project to file complaints in cases of job discrimination.

Since one of the project's goals is to increase employment opportunities for older women, it is presently involved in helping women establish business collectives.

Retirement Jobs, Inc.

730-C Distel Circle
Los Altos, CA 94022
415-965-2900

This nonprofit job referral service placed more than 11,000 persons in paid jobs last year alone. The variety of work is wide, from janitorial and home health aides to office clerks and accountants. About 30 percent of the jobs are full-time. A large portion of the jobs are with businesses, the balance are in home settings. Retirement Jobs also publishes a quarterly newsletter, and conducts a vigorous public relations effort.

Branch offices are located in the following California cities:

Alviso 95002
1568 Liberty Street
408-263-4688

Daly City 91724
6794 Mission Street
415-992-2567

East Menlo Park 94025
100 Terminal Avenue
415-327-9288

East San Jose 95116
50 King Road, S.
408-251-3003

Gilroy 95020
6th and Hanna Streets
408-842-4017

Los Gatos 95030
336C Village Lane
408-354-5171

Milpitas 95035
540 S. Abel Street
408-946-1774

Oakland 94612
401 Central Building
436 14th Street
415-444-7170

Palo Alto 94301
467 Hamilton Avenue
415-326-6180

Redwood City 94063
1050B Middlefield Road
415-364-4916

San Francisco 94108
251 Kearny Street
415-781-4831

San Jose 95113
210 1st Street, S.
408-294-3558

San Mateo 94403
190 25th Avenue, W.
415-574-4474

South San Jose 95123
5585 Cottle Road
408-578-2925

Sunnyvale 94086
Lockheed Building 560
Room 111
408-734-0276

Walnut Creek 94546
1327 N. Main Street
415-939-1550

Marin Senior Coordinating Council, Inc.

The Depot — 930 Tamalpais Avenue
San Rafael, CA 94901
415-461-1316

This free service places older persons in primarily part-time work. Most jobs are domestic, but persons have been placed as salespeople, drivers, security and maintenance personnel, accountants, bookkeepers, bank managers, and landscape architects.

Job Resource Center

2015 J Street
Sacramento, CA 95814

The center primarily serves disadvantaged women and finds employers reluctant to hire people over 55. Jobs are mostly clerical assistants of some kind, paid by the hour. "Due to the tight job market, we have many highly educated women looking for jobs and they are quite willing (out of necessity) to take any kind of job. We are trying to develop more opportunities in management and administration."

Senior Home Repair Service

Employment Development Department
1325 S Street
Sacramento, CA 95814
916-445-9118

Just what the name implies—part-time jobs for people with home-repair skills. The prevailing rate is $5.50 an hour and you must have your own transportation.

Careers for 50+ Employment Service
Kathryn Higgins
P.O. Box 4333
Stockton, CA 95204

Mostly part-time jobs in service industries for people in the San Joaquin County area.

Connecticut
Sage Advocate Employment Service
53 Wall Street
New Haven, CT 06510
203-777-7401

A nonprofit employment referral and counseling agency for people over 55. Sage Advocate, which has been in existence since 1972, reports a steady rise in opportunities, with a very sharp one in the past year with new interest on the part of employers in small businesses and industry. Fifty percent of the jobs are in the area of home care, baby-sitting, and kitchen help. The next largest demand is for skilled craftsmen from the building trades for home maintenance work. The rest of the jobs are for office workers and management or professional people. Most of the jobs are part-time. All pay at least the minimum wage.

Senior Personnel Placement Bureau
520 West Avenue
Norwalk, CT 06850
203-838-7553

Established in 1966, the bureau placed 167 people in mostly part-time jobs in 1977. The majority are in domestic work, but some are more unusual—the retired operator of a shrimp factory is now working in a library and the former owner of a bicycle shop is overseeing a restaurant operation.

Senior Employment Service, Inc.
1642 Bedfort Street, Room 107
Stamford, CT 06905
203-327-4422 and -5716

S.E.S. has in its files "hundreds of experi-

enced men and women over 55 whose skills and motivations are well above average." The job categories range from blue-collar to front-office executive, and although they try to place their top-level applicants in appropriate positions, it isn't often possible. The agency actively promotes the employment of older people with the business community through newsletters.

Waterbury Seniors Employment Service
235 Grand Street
Waterbury, CT 06702
203-547-6760

A relatively new organization, with mostly part-time placements—clerical, factory, bank security, companion, and domestic jobs.

West Hartford Seniors Job Bank, Inc.
50 S. Main
West Hartford, CT 06107

For job seekers 55 years old and over. Most of the 250 placements a year are in service, clerical, and retail jobs. They get calls for attorneys and consultants in a variety of fields. A local bank hired a retired state banking commissioner in a marketing position.

Delaware
Wilmington Senior Center Employment Services
Wilmington Senior Center
1901 N. Market Street
Wilmington, DE 19801
302-654-4441

Part-time jobs for older persons in areas such as maintenance, clerical, child care, and sales. One retiree conducts pre-retirement seminars for the AFL-CIO.

Florida
Senior Citizens Services, Inc.
940 Court Street
Clearwater, FL 33516
813-442-8104

Who's Looking for a Job?

A recent sample listing of job applicants at the Sage Advocate Employment Service in New Haven sheds some interesting light on the desire, as well as the need, of older people to work. Among the job applicants were:

A 65-year-old chemical engineer, who came to the office after one week of retirement.

An 83-year-old father of a Yale professor who had worked for sixty years as a pilot on small oil freighters.

The 70-year-old widow of a Congregational minister. ("Placed immediately.")

A 64-year-old former state police captain.

A 69-year-old former senior librarian from the art cataloguing department at Yale. Speaks four languages.

A 74-year-old retired cashier at a local restaurant.

A 60-year-old corporate secretary and credit manager, just laid off from the firm she had been with for thirty-five years.

A recent widow, age 59, looking for general office work.

A 69-year-old electrician and electrical cost analyst.

A 70-year-old writer, author of fourteen novels, with editing, reporting, and public relations experience, looking for part-time work.

Job offerings vary by season and economic conditions, but the service places more than 2000 people a year, slightly more than half of them men. Most of the jobs are part-time, although some experienced women have found full-time jobs. There is no shortage of jobs for sick-room aides and domestic workers. Jobs for men include part-time hotel and motel clerks.

Adult Assistance, Inc.

222 East Silver Springs Boulevard
Ocala, FL 32670
904-732-4393

This new job service for people over 55 placed 200 job-seekers in its first six months of operation. "Most of the people in our area know how to work—they don't know how to look for work." The agency's placements range from dishwashing jobs to executive positions.

"Many employers tell us that they like to hire people over 55 as they are more dependable. However, they don't always hire them! A ten-unit local filling station franchise is hiring only older workers for a period of four hours a day. They have hired many of our clients with sales and cashier experience, in some cases husband and wife teams."

Senior Citizens Guidance, Information, and Referral Service

709 Mirror Lake Drive, N.
St. Petersburg, FL 33701

The service is a department within the adult education program of Pinellas

County. Most jobs are in service industries or domestic work.

Georgia
Golden Age Employment Service
34 Tenth Street, N.E.
Atlanta, GA 30309
404-892-3209
and
140 E. Ponce de Leon Avenue
Decatur, GA 30030
404-377-0428
This agency serves people over 40.

Idaho
Retirement Jobs of Idaho, Inc.
700 Robbins Road
Boise, ID 83702
208-342-3605
Full- or part-time jobs for people 55 and older. Jobs for women include companion, child-care, secretarial, and other office work. Jobs for men include the building trades, bus driving, gardening, and hauling. An average of seventy to eighty people are placed each month.

Illinois
Suburban Cook County Area Agency on Aging
223 West Jackson Boulevard
Chicago, IL 60606
312-341-1400
The agency serves people 60 years old and over. In its first year of operation, it placed 1200 people in jobs ranging from janitorial to educational consultation. Almost all of the placements are part-time.

Berwyn Cicero Council on Aging
5817 W. Cermak Road
Cicero, IL 60650
312-863-3552
Most jobs are part-time or temporary, but there are some full-time placements. Older people have been placed as office workers, baby-sitters, companions, tool and die makers, printers, decorators, plumbers, electricians, TV repairmen, and factory workers.

South Suburban Council on Aging
15402 Center Avenue
Harvey, IL 60426
312-333-4988
This nonprofit agency offers free counseling and job placement to people 55 years old and over. Most jobs are part-time and include elderly and child care, janitorial, office work, and sales. Some unusual placements include a person hired as a Spanish tutor for someone traveling to Spain, and "mystery shoppers" hired by a department store to check on employees' handling of specific requests.

There is also Project Reentry, which provides employers with experienced temporary help, both office personnel and skilled employees. Project Reentry serves as the employer, handling payroll, taxes, insurance, and fringe benefits.

Senior Talent Employment Pool
Older Workers' Program
1303 N. Cunningham
Urbana, IL 61801
217-384-3768
Although most of the work is in the clerical and service fields, the program recently placed a 61-year-old blind man in a guidance counseling job.

Indiana
Senior Enterprises, Inc.
2 W. Vermont Street
Indianapolis, IN 46204
317-634-7007
The Homemaker service is the biggest division of this agency, which is funded by Title III of the Older Americans Act and monitored by the Central Indiana Council on Aging. The general employment division handles all kinds of jobs from administrators to security guards. Most requests are for labor and maintenance workers, and

clerical and secretarial jobs are the hardest to fill. However, a few people have been placed in managerial and administrative positions. One important aspect of the service is a monthly follow-up on both applicants and employees. During the most recent fiscal year, Senior Enterprises found 507 different jobs of at least one day's duration for 302 people. The total earned by these workers was $250,000.

REAL Services
622 N. Michigan Street
South Bend, IN 46634

Most jobs are part-time for low-income people aged 55 and older through the Senior Aides Program. However, a few full-time placements have been made outside of that program. Jobs run the gamut from custodial to administrative positions and include teachers' aides, secretaries, drivers, nurses' aides, and handymen.

Iowa
Retired Iowan Community Employment Program (RICEP)
(Offices in Ames, Burlington, Carroll, Cedar Rapids, Centerville, Chariton, Clinton, Council Bluffs, Creston, Davenport, Des Moines, Dubuque, Fort Dodge, Iowa City, Keokuk, Marshalltown, Mason City, Muscatine, Perry, Shenandoah, Sioux City, and Waterloo.)

RICEP is a state-funded program administered through the Iowa Department of Job Service, with offices in twenty-two communities. Look up the address in your local telephone book or write:
Job Services of Iowa
1000 E. Grand Avenue
Des Moines, IA 50319

The program is designed to bring awareness to older people about jobs and supportive services available to them. RICEP employs twenty older worker specialists, themselves at least 55 years old. They do registration, interviewing, counseling, refer-

ral, and placement. Other RICEP services include retraining, job development, and conducting pre-retirement and retirement programs.

Maryland
Over-60 Employment Counseling Service
309 N. Charles Street
Baltimore, MD 21201
301-752-7876

In fifteen years, the agency has placed 7200 people in jobs. Blue-collar work predominates, but office jobs range from clerical to executive. About 70 percent of the jobs are part-time.

Center for Displaced Homemakers
2435 Maryland Avenue
Baltimore, MD 21218
301-243-5000

and

Baltimore New Directions for Women
2517 North Charles Street
Baltimore, MD 21218
301-366-8570

A displaced homemaker is a woman who has worked most of her life for her family in the home and now—through death, divorce, or some other reason—having lost her income, would have trouble finding employment on her own. Several states, including Maryland, have passed Displaced Homemaker bills to help women in this position. The Center for Displaced Homemakers offers counseling, workshops, job training services, referrals to community resources, and other support services. Once women who come here are considered "job ready," they are referred to New Directions for Women, a career-counseling and job placement agency for women of all ages.

Over 60 Counseling and Employment Service
4700 Norwood Drive

Chevy Chase, MD 20015
301-652-8072

This service of the Montgomery County Federation of Women's Clubs is one of the oldest of its kind. In addition to finding jobs, Over 60 offers pre-retirement counseling and retraining for office work. In 1977, the office placed more than 1000 people in the Washington, D.C., area in work ranging from the unskilled to a $20,000-a-year engineer. Because the federal government hires most of the younger secretarial help available, Over 60 gets many calls for all kinds of office workers, from clerical to managerial. About 25 percent of the jobs are full-time, but the agency notes that in recent years more older people are taking full-time jobs and forfeiting their social security payments.

"Age discrimination in this country is very subtle," Over 60 says. "Larger corporations are mainly not interested in the older worker. This agency has had eighteen years of experience in placing older people and for the most part we have placed them with small businesses and nonprofit organizations. Our better work has been accomplished on a one-to-one basis, marketing specific skills for one individual at a time, which is very time consuming."

Over 60 also has a Senior Home Craftsman Program for people who want to turn a fix-it hobby into part-time paying work.

Michigan
Senior Services of Muskegon, Inc.

161 Muskegon Mall
Muskegon, MI 49440
616-722-3777

Charlotte Thornton, job placement specialist, reports she is seeing a trend among applicants who are "skilled, talented, and professional" lately. Jobs, however, tend to be part-time or temporary in clerical, sales, day care, home maintenance, housework, and teaching. Full-time employment is available for skilled craftsmen.

Missouri
Project ENCORE

Jewish Vocational Service
1608–12 Baltimore Avenue
Kansas City, MO 64108

The agency places about 250 people a year in all kinds of jobs, from managerial to custodial, and says there is a very definite interest on the part of employers in people over 55 — they have more job offers than they can fill. Among their placements:

A Methodist minister, released by his church after thirty-six years of service because of eye problems (although he can drive), got a job as manager of a rehabilitation center. A middle-management airline executive, fired at 55, was placed as manager of a travel agency.

For people between the ages of 55 and 62, most of the agency's placements are in full-time jobs; over 62, they are mostly part-time.

Project EARN

1727 Locust Street
St. Louis, MO 63103
314-241-3464

This counseling and placement service for people over 60 tries to place applicants according to their interests and abilities — in virtually all kinds of jobs except heavy industry. Most placements, however, are in service industries or personal service, since these are most available for people wanting part-time work to supplement their social security.

Project EARN has branch offices in Union, Washington, Pacific, De Soto, Arnold, St. Charles, and University City.

Nebraska
Jobs for Senior Citizens

900 N. 90th Street
Omaha, NE 68114

Most of the jobs pay minimum wage, in service industries, domestic work, clerical and secretarial, baby-sitting, and carpentry and other trades. The agency had a job order this year for a janitor for a worm farm—"We couldn't fill it but we had a few good laughs."

Nevada
Senior Citizens Employment Service
919 W. Bononga
Las Vegas, NV 89106

In March 1978, the service topped all its records and placed 156 people in jobs as accountants, clerks, hotel workers, baby-sitters, painters, plumbers, gardeners, handymen, typists, motel managers, cooks— "you name it, the whole spectrum." Most of the work is full-time, but may be of short duration.

Senior Employment Service
Nevada Catholic Welfare Bureau
275 E. 4th Street
Reno, NV 89513

Jobs for people 45 and older are mostly skilled work and full-time. Most of the placements are with business firms. The bureau placed almost 1000 people in 1977.

New Jersey
Essex County Senior Citizen Employment Bureau
160 Halstead Street
East Orange, NJ 07018
201-673-4252

The bulk of the agency's placements are people between the ages of 65 and 75. In the first six months of 1978, they interviewed 283 people and found jobs for slightly more than one third of them. "The market is still tight and employers are skeptical, but once they see how reliable and bright the seniors are, we have no trouble."

Work Center on Aging
Jewish Vocational Service
67 N. Clinton Street
East Orange, NJ 07017
201-674-2415

The Work Center on Aging is a nonsectarian, comprehensive vocational rehabilita-

tion program for mentally or physically disabled people over 55. People who are rehabilitated are placed in either private industry as clerical workers, messengers, drivers, salespeople, etc., or as permanent extended employees of the JVS sheltered workshop. In addition, the center attempts to place less severely handicapped people who do not require rehabilitation services.

Senior Personnel Registry (SPRY)
133 River Street
Hackensack, NJ 07601
201-489-7779

SPRY is a service for Bergen County residents, 60 and over. Most of the placements are in service, blue-collar, and clerical and sales jobs.

Senior Citizens Employment Bureau
60 Plus Center, YWCA
159 Glenridge Avenue
Montclair, NJ 07042

Most of the jobs are as domestic workers, companions, baby-sitters, and handymen, but this free service does place people in secretarial positions, as restaurant managers, drivers, typists, bank clerks, and receptionists.

This is one of the oldest employment services for older people in the country, and is reporting an increase in opportunities for older people. Most jobs are part-time, but temporary and full-time jobs are also filled. The bureau serves people over 55.

SAGE/OWL
50 DeForest Avenue
Summit, NJ 07901
201-273-5550

The Summit Area Association for Gerontological Endeavor employment referral service has been placing older men and women in jobs for the past ten years. Most jobs are part-time, and are in domestic positions, such as housekeepers, baby-sitters, and companions.

Older Americans Program Emphasizes Work

In 1977, under a three-year grant from the Edna McConnell Clark Foundation, the American Association of Community and Junior Colleges set up an Older Americans Program specifically geared to helping older adults remain in the work force.

The initial priority of the OAP is to encourage community colleges to recruit and hire older people in their own institutions. The second mandate asks community colleges to establish programs, training courses, and special workshops to assist older Americans to relocate in the job market or find substantive volunteer positions worthy of the mature persons' experiential background.

According to *Older Americans: New Uses of Mature Ability,* published by the OAP, "The most comprehensive way in which older people can be helped to realize their potential, and put it to use in the work role, is to provide the special counseling and job development services which address this older population's unique problems and concerns. Senior employment centers with professional and especially trained peer counselors provide the support system to the older job seeker. Job developers reach out to the community to help business and industry understand the benefits to be gained by hiring back or keeping middle aged and older people on the job."

For information on the program, write or call:

Jeanne B. Aronson, Director
Older Americans Program
American Association of Community and Junior Colleges
1 DuPont Circle, N.W.
Washington, DC 20036
202-293-7050

For a copy of *Older Americans: New Uses of Mature Ability,* send $3 to:

AACJC Publications
P.O. Box 298
Alexandria, VA 2314

New Mexico
Rent-a-Granny
610 Gold, S.W.
Albuquerque, NM 87102
505-243-7818

"Our people are in constant demand by public and private employers. Daily, we have jobs we cannot fill, which we turn over to other agencies." In spite of the name, the job placements are extremely varied.

In addition to being a placement service for people over 55, the agency offers supportive services, such as counseling, and housing and health referrals.

New York
PATH Program
Federation of the Handicapped
154 W. 14th Street
New York, NY 10011
212-242-5700

PATH's Older Worker Employment Division places job-ready men and women 55 and over. Older persons are placed in part-time and full-time jobs as clerical workers, bookkeepers, typists, receptionists, interpreters, salespersons, cashiers, managers, guards, and messengers.

Senior Personnel Employment Council of Westchester
158 Westchester Avenue
White Plains, NY 10601
914-761-2150

Founded in 1955, this service places persons over 60 in mostly part-time jobs. Commercial placements include clerks, secretaries, accountants, and general management jobs, as well as in the sales and industrial fields. Paid Neighbors are men and women who are placed as home companions, and Paid Grandmothers are persons who serve as sitters for children. Senior Temps provides temporary office help.

Branch offices are:

Senior Personnel Council of Northern Westchester
251 Lexington Avenue
Mount Kisco, NY 10549
914-666-7862

and

Senior Personnel of Fairview-Greenburgh
32 Manhattan Avenue
White Plains, NY 10607
914-682-5258

Senior Personnel Placement Bureau
22 Church Street
New Rochelle, NY 10805

Places about 200 people, 60 and over, each year in part-time domestic and industrial jobs.

Yonkers Employment Service for Seniors
36 S. Broadway
Yonkers, NY 10701
914-968-9320

This free employment service places persons 60 and over who register in approximately thirty-five job categories. Most of the jobs are part-time. Paid Neighbors are in constant demand. There are also many requests for clerical workers, bookkeepers, typists, baby-sitters, drivers, maintenance workers, porters, and salespeople.

Sixty Plus Employment Agency
10 North Broadway
Nyack, NY 10960
914-358-9391

This agency has mostly part-time jobs in all types of domestic, service, and clerical work.

GROW (Gaining Resources for Older Workers)
New York State Employment Office
40 Main Street
Binghamton, NY 13905
607-772-8770

GROW is a referral service that matches older persons seeking employment with individuals or businesses that need work done. GROW has made more than 1500 placements since its beginning in 1971. Most jobs are part-time, but there are requests for highly skilled and full-time workers. Placements have been made in small businesses, retail stores, and industrial firms. A large department store has provided forty persons with jobs, from switchboard operator to security guard. Others have been placed as housekeepers, companions, carpenters, painters, plumbers, and nurses' aides.

ACCORD

264 E. Onondaga Street
Syracuse, NY 13202
315-425-3436

ACCORD places persons 45 and over, usually in part-time jobs. Placements have been made in domestic work, bookkeeping, clerical, sales, and real estate. But there is an effort on the part of ACCORD to upgrade the types of jobs that employers ask for, so that professionals can be placed according to their education, expertise, and experience.

North Carolina
Cumberland County Coordinating Council on Older Adults

P.O. Box 36126
Florence Street
Fayetteville, NC 28303

Jobs are mostly full-time and in service industries.

North Dakota
Employment Security Bureau

1000 E. Divide Avenue
Bismarck, ND 58505
701-224-2837

The agency helps workers find suitable jobs, helps employers find workers, and provides unemployment insurance benefits. Employment services and manpower training programs are available through any branch office of the bureau without regard to race, color, creed, national origin, age, or sex. Services are provided at no charge to job seekers and employers.

The bureau gives emphasis in providing services to individuals experiencing difficulty in securing work or training because of age (generally 45 years of age and older). Employers are encouraged to remove age barriers.

There are fourteen branch offices in Bismarck, Devils Lake, Dickinson, Fargo, and Grafton. Write or call the main office for the address in your area.

Ohio
Skills Available Project

Security Federal Building
1110 Euclid Avenue
Cleveland, OH 44115
216-781-2944

The purpose of the Skills Available Project is to help older people to continue as members of the working population and to obtain employment regardless of age. Placements are made in all areas, from service to professional, with about 50 percent of the placements in part-time work. One man was hired, part-time, to watch a huge anniversary cake in a shopping mall. Recently Skills Available received a request for someone to carve Queen Anne legs for a custom-made harpsichord.

There are fifteen offices in Lorain County. Write or call for the address of the branch in your area.

Senior Citizens Placement Bureau of Franklin County

880 E. Broad Street
Columbus, OH 43205

This service arranges interviews between people aged 55 and over and employers seeking their experience and skills. In five years of operation, the bureau has placed more than 2000 people, mostly in part-time jobs with small businesses. Older persons have been placed as secretaries, draftsmen, mail clerks, food handlers, guards, typists, drivers, and salespeople.

Council on Aging of Warren County, Inc.

Senior Job Registry
300 North Broadway
Lebanon, OH 45036

The Senior Job Registry is a year old and serves people over 60. Since Warren County is a rural area with no public transportation, the agency's problem is finding jobs close to home. Other than that, they say, they have no difficulty in matching workers and jobs.

Oregon
Josephine County Senior Programs

317 N.W. B Street
Grants Pass, OR 97526
503-476-8201

Most placements are domestic, part-time, and low-skill. A few are funded by CETA.

Pennsylvania
Bethlehem Senior Citizens Council, Inc.

70 E. Broad Street
Bethlehem, PA 18018

The agency acts as a referral service only, for people over 55. Most of the jobs are part-time in service industries.

Tennessee
Senior Employment Service of Senior Neighbors, Inc.

10th and King Streets
Chattanooga, TN 37403
615-756-5950

The majority of jobs are part-time, in domestic work such as yard work, carpentry, and home companions, but placements have been made in all areas. One retired $40,000-a-year executive, bored with retirement, now works for minimum wage driving a "Pill Wagon" four hours a day, and loves it. Another man, who owned his own construction company for forty years, now works with a carpet and home cleaning company.

Senior Citizens Services, Inc.

3373 Poplar Avenue, Suite 401
Memphis, TN 38111
901-454-6835

Senior Citizens Services places persons 55 and over in part-time jobs through the federally funded Senior Aides Program. Jobs are in community service organizations, and the Senior Aides work twenty hours per week. (See page 103.)

Lewis Center for Senior Citizens

1188 N. Parkway
Memphis, TN 38105
901-272-7408

This center places between sixty and seventy people a month in mostly part-time jobs ranging from domestic and handyman work to professional positions.

Senior Citizens

1801 Broadway
Nashville, TN 37203
615-327-4551

Job placements for people 55 and older run about thirty-five a month, mostly part-time. Half the jobs are in industry, half in domestic work.

Texas
Senior Employment Service

307 Marshall Street
San Antonio, TX 78212
512-222-1294

Begun as a volunteer organization in 1968, the Senior Employment Service is now a United Way agency with a paid director and ten volunteer workers. Older persons are placed in every job classification, both skilled and unskilled. Jobs have included maintenance, sales, practical

Salesmen Improve with Age

The mandatory retirement policies of other companies have served the Texas Refinery Corporation of Fort Worth well. "Every time they let someone go because of age," says Adlai M. Pate, Jr., chairman of the board, "I have another potential salesperson.

"Like good wine, good salespeople improve with age," explains Tate, who ought to know. Texas Refinery has 400 people in its "Sizzling Sixties" club and they have the best sales records in the company.

nurses, cooks, carpenters, electricians, secretaries, machinists, mechanics, baby-sitters, and live-in companions. About 50 percent of the jobs are part-time. One man with a law degree and a CPA degree had two eye transplants, so to save his eyes he took a job in an advisory capacity in a local business. A recently widowed woman felt she could do nothing useful. Senior Employment Service discovered she had done sewing for her family all her life, and placed her in a San Antonio dress shop doing alterations.

Virginia
Senior Citizens Employment and Services of Alexandria, Inc.
121 N. St. Asaph Street
Alexandria, VA 22314
703-836-4414

Serves people over 60 who live in Alexandria and adjacent Fairfax County. Since Alexandria has a very low unemployment rate, the agency has more jobs than applicants to fill them. Most of the jobs are part-time and half are in domestic work.

Arlington County Job Development Service
Senior Adult Section
2100 14th Street N.
Arlington, VA 22201

The senior adult section specializes in counseling and placing individuals 55 and over. The job market for this group is excellent for companions to the elderly, child care, and minor home repairs; good for desk clerks, security guards, and bookkeepers, but poor for professionals who want to stay in their fields. A retired foreign-service officer with a great interest in woodwork was placed as a custom picture framer at an art gallery; a retired technical writer got a job with a consulting firm writing and editing grant requests, and a retired teacher of accounting was placed as a bookkeeper with a local hot line.

Senior Adult Employment Service
Fairfax County Department of
  Manpower Services
5633 Leesburg Pike
Bailey's Crossroads, VA 22041
703-671-0414

Serves people 55 and older in McLean, Reston, Vienna, Springfield, and Bailey's Crossroads.

Senior Services Employment Office
18 N. King Street
Leesburg, VA 22075

Serves residents of Loudoun County who are over 55. Most of the placements are secretarial, in retail businesses, security, and domestic work. At present the agency has more requests from employers than it can fill.

League of Older Americans, Inc.

401 Campbell Avenue, S.W.
Roanoke, VA 24016
703-981-1486

Makes all types of job placements, but most are blue-collar and domestic.

Washington
Older Worker Placement Service

Bellingham Senior Center
315 Halleck
Bellingham, WA 98225

OWPS is a joint effort of the Washington State Employment Security Department and the Whatcom County Council on Aging, and provides employment services to older people. Most placements are part-time or temporary. Jobs have been found for handymen, yard workers, companions, housekeepers, and janitors as well as skilled workers such as plumbers, carpenters, and bookkeepers.

Senior Employment Program

Senior Services of Snohomish County
3402 112th, S.W.
Everett, WA 98204
toll-free number 1-800-562-3931

Most jobs are in service industries. In 1977, they made 235 permanent, 561 temporary, and 1023 "casual" placements. The program has offices in senior centers in Everett, Edmonds, Arlington, and Monroe. Telephone the main office for the addresses in your community.

Skagit County Senior Services

403 Myrtle Street
Mount Vernon, WA 98273

Part-time and occasional jobs for persons 55 and over. Placements include domestic work, chores, yard work, library aide, bookkeeper, etc.

Senior Workers Service

West 300 Mission Avenue
Spokane, WA 99201
509-456-2734

This free employment service provides part-time and temporary employment to persons over 55. There are more than 400 people in their Job Bank File, and last year the Senior Workers Service received more than 3000 requests from employers. Most placements are in such areas as maintenance, home repair, drivers, companions, and yard work. But some are for clerical, sales, skilled trades, and professional work.

Clark County Senior Employment Program

301 E. 17th Street
Vancouver, WA 98660

A free service to anyone 55 and older, this program places older persons in a variety of jobs such as accounting and bookkeeping, motel management, carpentry, sales, landscaping, computer services, forestry, painting, and domestic work. Both part-time and full-time placements are made.

Counseling on types of employment and sources of information about jobs is also available.

The program cooperates with other employment agencies in the area, as well as with the Employment Security Office and CETA, so that applicants may have the advantage of all possibilities throughout the community.

Placements are also made in federally funded job programs, including the Foster Grandparent Program, Senior Companions, and Green Thumb.

Wisconsin
"Help When Needed" Services

Consumers Co-op
2221 Highland Avenue
Eau Claire, WI 54701
715-839-2840

Mostly part-time jobs in service and domestic work. The agency, which has been in operation since 1974, is sponsored by the Eau Claire City-County Association on Aging.

Over 55 Employment Service
822 E. Johnson, #5
Madison, WI 53703
608-255-5585

Provides employment counseling, job development, and placement services to adults 55 and older residing in Dane County. Call the main office for the telephone number of branch offices in your area. This is one of the rare agencies that wrote, "We have encountered tremendous cooperation on the part of employers." The jobs, mostly part-time, are "as varied as a metropolitan market can provide." They include professional business consulting, medical assistance, secretarial, social services, clerical, and maintenance work, with quite a few opportunities with the University of Wisconsin.

Part III

Keeping Fit

CHAPTER 8

Exercise

Within the past few years, exercise programs for older people have been started in virtually every major American city—in one year alone, the sixty-six-year-old Executive Director of the President's Council on Physical Fitness, C. Carson Conrad, conducted workshops for 140,000 volunteer leaders of fitness programs. If there is a fountain of youth, the late–twentieth century guide to finding it is through exercise.

If you cannot, or don't want to, join a regular exercise class, this chapter contains a personal exercise regimen that you can follow at home. It was designed by the President's Council on Physical Fitness and the Administration on Aging, and is the nearest thing to an official exercise program for older people that exists. If you are reading this as a library book, or you want extra copies for friends, you can order the booklet from the Superintendent of Documents. (See note at the end of this chapter.)

The Importance of Exercise

Most medical authorities support the belief—and most active people experience the fact—that exercise helps a person look, feel, and work better.

Various organs and systems of the body, particularly the digestive process, are stimulated through activity and as a result work more effectively.

Posture can be improved through proper exercise by increasing the tone of supporting muscles. This not only improves appearance but can decrease the frequency of lower back pain and disability.

Physically active individuals are less likely to experience a heart attack or other forms of cardiovascular disease than sedentary people. And apparently an active person who does suffer a coronary attack will probably have a less severe form and will be more apt to survive the experience.

Physical activity is as important as diet in maintaining proper weight. And being overweight is more than a matter of individual discomfort. It is related to several chronic diseases, shortened live expectancy, and emotional problems. Medical authorities now recommend that weight reduction be accomplished by a reasonable increase in daily physical activity, supplemented, if necessary, by proper dietary controls.

Exercise can't prevent the stresses of life, but it can help you cope with them. For many individuals, frequent involvement in some sort of physical activity helps to reduce mental fatigue, tension, strain, or boredom produced by our mechanized and sedentary way of life.

There is an advantage also in keeping fit and maintaining your physical capabilities to meet conditions caused by illness or accident. The person who has good control of his body and physical reserves is much better equipped to cope with such problems and to follow a rehabilitative program if he should have to do so.

The physically active and able person usually has a positive feeling about himself. He or she also possesses a degree of physical courage that propels him or her into interesting and stimulating experiences; moves with grace and ease; and generally presents a trim, attractive, and self-confident bearing.

Perhaps the greatest benefit of maintaining physical fitness is the degree of independence it affords. This is a quality to be most prized in the later years. There is a great psychological and financial advantage in having the ability to plan and do things without depending upon relatives, friends, or hired help. To drive your own car, to succeed with do-it-yourself projects rather than trying to find and pay someone else for the service, to go and come as you please, to be an aid rather than a liability in emergencies—these are forms of personal freedom well worth working for.

How Exercise Promotes Dynamic Fitness

Efficiency and Endurance of the Heart and Lungs

The proper working of the heart, lungs, and blood vessels is probably the most important aspect of fitness in the adult years. Vital to good

Sanford Yoelson leads an exercise class at Bronx House in New York City.

fitness are a strong and responsive heart that can pump the blood needed to nourish billions of body cells, good lungs where gases of cell metabolism are exchanged for life-giving oxygen, and elastic blood vessels free of obstructions. Activities involving leg muscles help maintain good circulation by the squeezing action of the muscles on the veins. This benefit cannot be achieved by any other means. More and more evidence from scientific research points to the importance of regular physical activity in maintaining good circulation and respiration.

Muscular Strength and Endurance

Muscles grow in size and strength only if they are used. They grow soft and flabby and lose their strength and elasticity if they are not used.

While strength does decrease with advancing years, the rate of decline can be lessened by keeping the muscles toned through regular exercise. Strength and endurance can be promoted by increasing the number of times an exercise is performed, by adding more weight or friction, and by increasing the speed of movement.

Balance

The balance mechanism of the body is commonly neglected and yet is extremely important in the fitness of older people. The balance mechanism is maintained through use and degenerates when not used.

Many older people tend to lose their sense of balance much more quickly than nature intended. The need to use bifocal or trifocal glasses increases the hazards for many. A well-maintained sense of balance can help make up for the problems caused by quick changes in vision from one optical focus to another.

Flexibility

The ability to move the joints through their normal range of motion is important, but here again the aging process and disuse cause the tissues surrounding the joints to increase in thickness and lose their elasticity. Moving the joints in a proper exercise program can delay this process. Exercise of the joints also helps slow down the onset or the development of arthritis, one of the most common and painful diseases associated with old age. Proper exercise that stretches the muscles can help keep them supple and prevent them from becoming short and tight.

Traditional concern for older people has perhaps done them a disservice. The idea has been to put the push buttons in easy reach, to keep the shelves low, to avoid necessity for bending and stretching. Instead, older people should be encouraged to bend, move, and stretch in order to keep joints flexible, muscles springy, and the heart feeling young.

Coordination and Agility

A well-coordinated individual should be able to direct parts of the body in skillful movement, to coordinate different actions with each other and with the eyes, to move and change directions quickly and safely.

Highly refined skills may not be essential in the later years. But for enjoyment of recreation and to keep in condition to move freely and safely, you should exercise regularly in order to maintain reasonably good levels of coordination and agility.

Principles of Exercise and Fitness Programming

Physical fitness can be improved by gradually increasing the amount of work performed, but it is necessary to progress in easy stages. The enthusiast who tackles a keep-fit program too fast and too strenuously soon gives up in discomfort, if not in injury.

While some activity has to be sustained to obtain major benefits, the cumulative effect of exercises and activities carried on during a period of time counts. For example, every movement uses calories, so the way to burn up calories is to move. And even though certain actions—such as a short walk—may not use many calories at the time, a number of short walks in the course of a day can use up a fair-sized total. Similarly, the benefits of movement to the organs, the joints, and the muscles add up little by little.

Therefore, try to step up activity throughout your day, in addition to following specifically planned periods of exercise.

At all ages, but increasingly in later years, it is important to prepare your body for vigorous activity by warming up. Any individual, and especially an older person, should definitely avoid suddenly undertaking a strenuous activity. A warm-up period should be performed by starting lightly with a continuous rhythmical activity such as walking and gradually increasing the intensity until your pulse rate, breathing, and body temperature are elevated. It is also desirable to do some easy stretching, pulling, and rotating exercises during the warm-up period.

Swimming is good exercise, but these Bronx House members don't let it interrupt a lively discussion.

Periods of vigorous activity should be alternated with periods of lesser stress. Put the pressure on for a while and then release it. By gradually increasing the stressful interval and reducing the less vigorous interval, you improve your physical condition. This principle of interval training can be applied to many forms of exercise and is particularly adaptable to walking, jogging, and swimming.

The proper way to advance in strength and physical condition is to put increasing workloads on your system. This is called the *overload principle*. Challenge yourself little by little toward improved performance by increasing the amount of exercise performed or the speed at which you perform it. For example, if you repeat an exercise five times, a certain amount of work has been done and value derived. The next step is to perform the exercise six times, and then gradually increase the count until you can do it, say, ten times with ease.

Unless the overload principle is employed, only minimal gains will be achieved. This is why it is important to follow a graduated, progressive schedule. This principle applies to the circulatory system as well as to the voluntary muscles. To increase the efficiency of the heart and lungs, the performance of continuous rhythmic exercise for a period long enough to stress the circulatory system is recommended—brisk walking, jogging, bicycling, swimming, rope skipping, or the like. Action should be increased until it can be sustained hard and long enough to keep the pulse rate above 130 for several minutes and to increase the body temperature gradually to the point of perspiration. Programs that promise fitness in a minute a day are less than adequate in their effect on circulation. So, too, are the traditionally recommended activities for the elderly, such as puttering in the garden or taking a leisurely stroll.

Dos and Don'ts for Older People

Before you start *any* kind of exercise program, carefully read these Dos and Don'ts offered by Mr. Conrad.

* DO listen to your body. It will tell you when you're doing too much. If you become winded or over tired while exercising, switch to a less demanding activity or one that uses a different set of muscles. Letting yourself become winded can place a strain on your heart.

* DO warm up for several minutes before doing more difficult exercises. This will help the circulatory and respiratory systems adjust to the increased level of activity and also help avoid injuries to the muscles and connective tissues. If you engage in a really strenuous activity

such as running, you also should cool down by walking until pulse and breathing return to normal levels.

* DO exercise at least three times a week on a regular schedule. If you work out at the same time on all of your exercise days, exercise tends to become a natural part of your daily routine, much like bathing or brushing your teeth.

* DO strive for a good balance in your workout with flexibility, strength, and endurance exercises. All are important to fitness.

* DO gradually increase your workload. Improvements in fitness are made by gradually extending the limits of performance.

* DO stand tall and erect, with the stomach in and hips forward, when exercising. This will keep the body in proper alignment, improve muscle tone, and help you avoid joint problems. It also will improve your outlook on life.

* DO take ten deep breaths four or five times a day to increase lung capacity.

* DO hold on to some support, such as the back of a chair, when doing exercises that involve the possibility of losing balance.

* DON'T compete with others to see who can do the most exercise. Work at your own level and speed to avoid strain and gradually improve performance.

* DON'T engage in activities that require quick, jerky movements without first undergoing a long period of conditioning. Sudden exertion can lead to injury and unnecessary strain.

* DON'T be a weekend warrior, a person who tries to squeeze all of his exercise into a couple of days. Many of the benefits of exercise can be stored for only two days, and regular participation is the key to lasting gains.

* DON'T push yourself to the point of exhaustion. Exercise at a rate that elevates the pulse and breathing, and that causes you to perspire lightly, but stop short of being winded and weak.

* DON'T take a sauna or steam bath after exercise. This places an additional burden on the heart, which already is busy supplying the extra oxygen used during exercise. A sauna or steam bath followed by a cool shower *before* exercise is okay.

* DON'T sell yourself short. Most older persons underestimate their physical capabilities. There are many strong distance runners and swimmers who are in their 70s. They are people who have observed the rules outlined briefly here.

The Exercise Program

Finding Your Exercise Level

In this reasonable exercise program planned for you, there are three series of exercises, graded according to their difficulty or the amount of stress involved. They are identified as the A, B, and C programs, with A the easiest, B next, and C the most difficult and sustained. They let you start where you should, and they provide an easy progression as you improve your physical condition.

Each of these three exercise programs is designed to give you a balanced workout, utilizing all major muscle groups. Performing your program regularly will lead to improvement in the various components of physical fitness, especially in the functioning of the heart and lungs.

As you grow proficient at the exercises in your program, you should increase the number of repetitions of certain exercises, and increase the duration and speed of walking and jogging.

As you become able to increase the number of repetitions and handle more complicated and demanding exercises, you can move up to the next level with new confidence and a growing feeling of well-being.

Which Series?

How do you know where to start? Are you at level A, B, or C?

First, you should ask your physician for advice. Discuss your plans with your own doctor (or public-health clinic physician) and follow his recommendations. Take this book along to show him. Ask him to review the program recommended here and to advise you accordingly. Also give yourself the following simple tests to determine your present condition and your exercise tolerance. In other words, find out just what kind of shape you are in.

The tests will help you select your appropriate exercise level and pace. Keep in mind that there are wide variations in physical performance. Your own individual physical condition must dictate your personal exercise program.

Check yourself in easy stages. First, try the walk test below.

Walk Test

The idea behind this walk test is to determine how many minutes, up to ten, you can walk briskly on a level surface without undue difficulty or discomfort. Test yourself outdoors preferably, but walking around the room indoors will do if necessary.

If you can finish three minutes but no more, you should begin your daily exercise program with level A.

If you can go beyond three minutes but not quite to ten minutes, you can *warm up* at level A for a week or two, and then move up to level B.

If you can breeze through the whole ten minutes, you are ready for bigger things. Rest awhile, or wait until the next day, and then take the Walk-Jog Test #1.

One note of caution. If at any time during the Walk Test you experience any trembling, nausea, extreme breathlessness, pounding in the head, or pain in the chest, STOP immediately. These are signs that you have reached your present level of exercise tolerance. Start your keep-fit program at the corresponding level described in relation to this test. If these symptoms *persist* beyond a point of temporary discomfort, check with your physician.

Walk-Jog Test #1
This test consists of alternately walking fifty steps and jogging fifty steps for a total of six minutes. Read instructions under Exercise #2 on page 136 before undertaking this test.

Walk at the rate of 120 steps per minute; that is, your left foot strikes the ground once each second. *Jog* at the rate of 144 steps per minute; your left foot hits the ground eighteen times every fifteen seconds. Time your walking and jogging intervals for fifteen seconds occasionally to check your pace.

If you stop this test before the six minutes are up, plan your schedule of exercises at level B.

If you complete the six-minute walk-jog test without difficulty, you can probably undertake level C. It might be well to *warm up* for a week or two on the B program first, however.

If you can perform this test without difficulty and feel you are capable of a more rigorous trial, rest a day, and then take the Walk-Jog Test #2.

Walk-Jog Test #2
This test consists of alternately walking 100 steps and jogging 100 steps for a total of ten minutes. Follow the directions and use the same rates of speed—walking and jogging—as described for Walk-Jog Test #1.

If you complete this ten-minute test without difficulty, you can obviously handle the C program in this book, and might want to consider going beyond it to more advanced exercises.

If you do not complete the ten-minute walk-jog, warm up for a few days on program B and then go on to program C.

Keep an Exercise Schedule

Now that you've tested yourself and determined where to begin, schedule a definite period for your basic exercises every day and stick with it.

This means setting aside thirty minutes to an hour a day for a planned program of physical activity. You should consider your exercises to be just as important as eating a proper diet or keeping clean.

General Directions—All Levels

The exercises in this program are not graded separately for men and women but are tailored to individuals. A couple can do the exercises together. More than likely, however, a man who has been active can start at a higher level or progress faster than most of the women who undertake the program.

Begin *very slowly* and increase the tempo and number of repetitions *very gradually*. This will keep stiffness and soreness to a minimum. If you do get a little stiff during the first few days, don't let it slow you down; the stiffness will soon be overcome and it is an indication that you *needed* the activity.

Follow the directions for your exercise exactly. If, for example, you are at level A and a particular exercise should be performed only twice as a starter, stop after two repetitions—even though you may feel you can do many more. A warm-up is built into each exercise series. Therefore, the exercises should be performed in the order presented to give best results.

Keep a record of the exercises you perform, and how many times you repeat them. The little extra time required to keep a record of your activities and to set more and more challenging goals for yourself is well spent. A fitness program should be carefully designed and carefully followed. The best way to keep track of each day's performance is to write it down. The exercise schedules outlined in this book will be more beneficial to you if you keep good records.

One way of adding to the fun of your exercise program is to play music while you are exercising. You can select lively tunes and find music that fits the tempo of the various movements. This is particularly interesting when walking or jogging indoors. Some people also enjoy exercising while watching TV.

You can exercise with family and friends. Many groups get together in each other's homes or at a local center or club.

Wear comfortable clothing. Avoid tight-fitting, restrictive clothes, although, if you feel more comfortable wearing foundation garments, do so. Shorts or slacks, T-shirts or short-sleeved blouses are usually desirable. Wear well-fitting shoes with nonslip soles and low (or no) heels.

Specific Instructions for Individual Programs

The A Program

Try to complete the entire sequence without undue rest periods between exercises, but, of course, rest awhile if you feel overtaxed. One indication of improvement in condition is the ability to go through the workout in less and less time (up to a point), doing the exercises at a faster pace and resting for shorter periods between exercises. However, never let the effort to increase speed cause jerky movements or otherwise interfere with the correct performance of the exercise.

For the first week at least, perform only the smallest number of repetitions for the shortest duration of time shown under the illustration for each exercise. If you find even this amount to be strenuous, or if you feel fatigued at the end of the week, do not increase the repetitions or duration but continue at the same pace for another week.

After the first week—or as you are ready—in each exercise where a range of repetitions is shown, increase the minimum by *one*. Do this number, but no more, the second week. (If you need to stay at the lowest count, as explained above, don't increase the count at all.) In the following weeks, gradually increase the number of repetitions as you feel you can. Most people should take three to four weeks to reach the highest counts in the A program.

After you reach the point where you can do the higher number of repetitions shown for each exercise, continue on level A until you can complete the whole series without resting between exercises.

When you can do this for three days in a row, move on to level B.

The B Program

When you are ready to undertake level B, proceed in a fashion similar to your A program. That is, start at the lowest frequency of repetitions and gradually work up.

Most people should remain at level B for three to five weeks before moving on to C.

After you pass your "prove out" test by performing all of the B exercises at the highest frequency shown without resting in between for three consecutive workouts, move on to level C.

The C Program

Follow the same directions as for the A and B programs. Start slowly; step up activity gradually.

When you reach the upper limits of the C exercises and can go through the workout without stopping on three days in a row, you are ready to tackle bigger things. At this point you can (1) continue with the exercises in this book, gradually increasing the number and speed of repetitions, the distances walked and jogged, and also engage in more sports and recreational activities; or (2) obtain a copy of *Adult Physical Fitness—A Program for Men and Women,* which includes more difficult exercises. To order, send thirty-five cents to the U.S. Government Printing Office; the address is at the end of this chapter.

Important Note: Most, but NOT ALL, of the exercises illustrated on the next pages are included in all three exercise programs—the A, B, and C; but the same order IS NOT followed in the three programs.

Do only those exercises included in your program level.

Perform your exercises in the order indicated for your program.

Order of Exercises
The A Program Sequence
Walk (2 minutes)
Bend and Stretch
Rotate Head
Body Bender
Wall Press
Arm Circles
Wing Stretcher
Walk (2–5 minutes)
Lying Leg Bend
Angel Stretch
Walk a Straight Line
Half Knee Bend
Wall Push-Away
Side Leg Raise
Head and Shoulder Curl
Alternate Walk (50 steps) Jog (10 steps), 1–3 minutes
Walk (1–3 minutes)

The B Program Sequence
Walk (3 minutes)
Bend and Stretch
Rotate Head

Body Bender
Wall Press
Arm Circles
Half Knee Bend
Wing Stretcher
Wall Push-Away
Walk (5 minutes)
Lying Leg Bend
Angel Stretch
Walk-the-Beam (2- by 6-inch beam)
Knee Push Up
Side Leg Raise
Head and Shoulder Curl (arms crossed on chest)
Diver's Stance
Alternate Walk (50 steps) Jog (25 steps), 3–6 minutes
Walk (1–3 minutes)

The C Program Sequence
Alternate Walk (50 steps) Jog (50 steps), 3 minutes
Bend and Stretch
Rotate Head
Body Bender

Wall Press
Arm Circles
Half Knee Bend
Wing Stretcher
Alternate Walk (50 steps) Jog (50
    steps), 3 minutes
Leg Raise and Bend
Angel Stretch
Walk-the-Beam (2- by 4-inch beam)
Hop
Knee Push Up
Side Leg Raise
Head and Shoulder Curl (hands clasped
    behind neck)
Stork Stand
Alternate Walk (50 steps) Jog (50
    steps), 5 minutes, gradually increas-
    ing to walk 100 steps, jog 100 steps
Walk (3 minutes)

Exercises

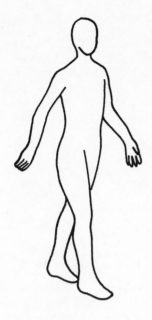

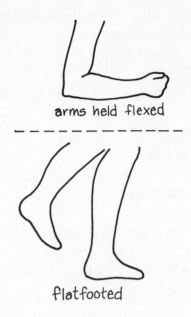

1. Walk

A   *2 minutes*
B   *3 minutes*

Starting position: Stand erect, balanced on balls of feet.

Action: Simply begin walking briskly on a level space, preferably outdoors, but walking around the room will do if necessary.

Value: A good warm-up exercise, loosening muscles, and preparing you for your full exercise schedule.

2. Alternate Walk-Jog

C   *only at this time*
Alternately walk 50 steps and jog 50—for about 3 minutes.

Starting position: As for walking, arms held flexed, forearms generally parallel to the ground.

Action: Jogging is a form of slow running. Begin walking for 50 steps, then shift to a slow run with easy strides, landing lightly each time on the heel of the foot and transfer weight to the whole foot in flatfooted style. (Heel-toe running in contrast to the sprint in which the runner stays on balls of his feet.) Arms should move loosely and freely from the shoulders in opposition to legs. Breathing should be deep but not labored to point of gasping.

Value: Good warm-up for more advanced exercises. Good for legs and circulation.

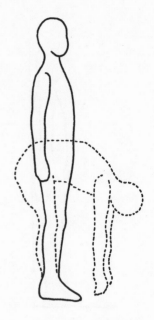

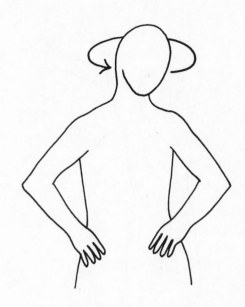

3. Bend and Stretch

A *Repeat 2 to 10 times*
B *Repeat 10 times*
C *Repeat 10 times*

Starting position: Stand erect, feet shoulder-width apart.

Action: *Count 1.* Bend trunk forward and down, flexing knees. Stretch gently in attempt to touch fingers to toes or floor. *Count 2.* Return to starting position.

Note: Do slowly, stretch and relax at intervals rather than in rhythm.

Value: Helps loosen and stretch most muscles of body; helps relaxation; aids in warm-up for more vigorous exercise.

4. Rotate Head

A *Repeat 2 to 10 times each way*
B *Repeat 10 times each way*
C *Repeat 10 times each way*

Starting position: Stand erect, feet shoulder-width apart; hands on hips.

Action: *Count 1.* Slowly rotate the head in a full circle from left to right. *Count 2.* Slowly rotate head in the opposite direction.

Note: Use slow, smooth motion, close eyes to help avoid losing balance or getting dizzy.

Value: Helps loosen and relax muscles of the neck, and firm up throat and chin line.

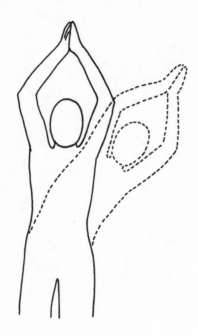

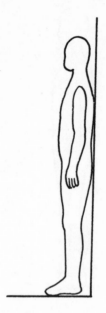

5. Body Bender

A *Repeat 2 to 5 times*
B *Repeat 5 to 10 times*
C *Repeat 10 times*

Starting position: Stand with feet shoulder-width apart, hands extended overhead, finger-tips touching.

Action: *Count 1.* Bend trunk slowly sideward to left as far as possible, keeping hands together and arms straight (don't bend elbows). *Count 2.* Return to starting position. *Counts 3 and 4.* Repeat to the right.

Value: Stretches arm, trunk, and leg muscles.

6. Wall Press

A *Repeat 2 to 5 times*
B *Repeat 5 times*
C *Repeat 5 times*

Starting position: Stand erect, head not bent forward or backward, back against wall, heels about 3 inches away from wall.

Action: *Count 1.* Pull in the abdominal muscles and press the small of the back tight against the wall. Hold for six seconds. *Count 2.* Relax and return to starting position.

Note: Keep entire back in contact with wall on *Count 1* and do not tilt the head backward.

Value: Promotes good body alignment and posture. Strengthens abdominal muscles.

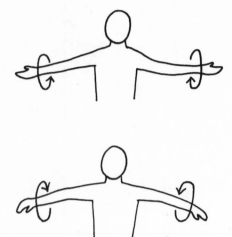

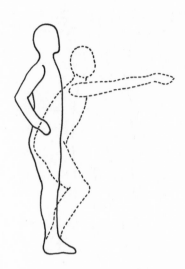

7. Arm Circles

A *Repeat 5 each way*
B *Repeat 5 to 10 each way*
C *Repeat 10 to 15 each way*

Starting position: Stand erect, arms extended sideward at shoulder height, palms up.

Action: Describe small circles backward with hands. Keep head erect. Reverse, turn palms down and do circles forward.

Value: Helps keep shoulder joint flexible; strengthens muscles of shoulders.

8. Half Knee Bend

A *Skip this exercise at this time.*
B *Repeat 5 to 10 times*
C *Repeat 10 to 15 times*

Starting position: Stand erect, hands on hips.

Action: *Count 1.* Bend knees halfway while extending arms forward, palms down. Keep heels on floor. *Count 2.* Return to starting position.

Value: Firms up leg muscles and stretches muscles in front of legs. Helps improve balance.

Note: *At this point in sequence* **A** *now return to Walk (Exercise #1) and walk 2 to 5 minutes;* **C** *return to Alternate Walk-Jog (Exercise #2) and walk 50 steps, jog 50 for 3 minutes.*

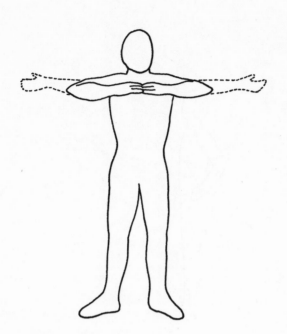

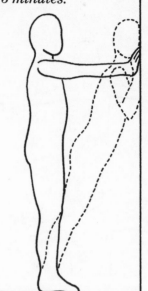

9. Wing Stretcher

A   *Repeat 2 to 5 times*
B   *Repeat 5 to 10 times*
C   *Repeat 10 to 20 times*

Starting position: Stand erect, bend arms in front of chest, extended finger tips touching and elbows at shoulder height. *Counts 1, 2, 3.* Pull elbows back as far as possible, keeping arms at shoulder height and returning to starting position each time. *Count 4.* Swing arms outward and sideward, shoulder height, palms up and return to starting position.

Note: This is a bouncy, rhythmic action, counting "one-and-two-and-three-and-four."

Value: Strengthens muscles of upper back and shoulders; stretches chest muscles. Helps promote good posture and prevent "dowager hump."

10. Wall Push-Away

B   *only at this time*
Repeat exercise 10 times; then walk for 5 minutes.

Starting position: Stand erect, feet about six inches apart, facing a wall, and arms straight in front, palms on wall, bearing weight slightly. *Count 1.* Bend elbows and lower body slowly toward wall, meanwhile turning head to the side, until cheek almost touches the wall. *Count 2.* Push against wall with the arms and return to the starting position.

Note: Keep heels on floor throughout the exercise.

Value: Increases strength of arm, shoulder, and upper-back muscles. Stretches muscles in chest and back of legs.

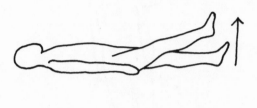

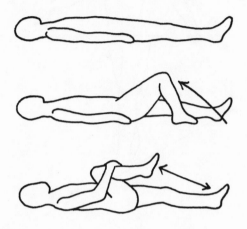

11. Lying Leg Bend

A *Repeat 2 to 5 times, each leg*
B *Repeat 5 to 10 times, each leg*
C *Skip this exercise*

Starting position: Lie on back, legs extended, feet together, arms at sides.

Action: *Count 1.* Bend left knee and move left foot toward buttocks, keeping foot in light contact with floor. *Count 2.* Move knee toward chest as far as possible, using abdominal, hip, and leg muscles; *then* clasp knee with both hands and pull slowly toward chest. *Count 3.* Return to position at end of *Count 1. Count 4.* Return to starting position.

Note: After completing desired number of repetitions with left leg, repeat the exercise using right leg.

Value: Improves flexibility of knee and hip joints; and strengthens abdominal and hip muscles.

12. Leg Raise and Bend

C *only*
Repeat 2 to 5 times. After completing desired number with left leg, do exercise with right leg.

Starting position: Lie on back, legs extended, feet together, arms at sides.

Action: *Count 1.* Raise extended left leg about 12 inches off the floor. *Count 2.* Bend knee and move knee toward chest as far as possible, using abdominal, hip, and leg muscles; *then* clasp knee with both hands and pull slowly toward chest. *Count 3.* Return to position at end of *Count 1. Count 4.* Return to starting position.

Value: Improves flexibility of knee and hip joints; strengthens abdominal muscles.

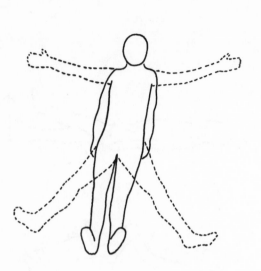

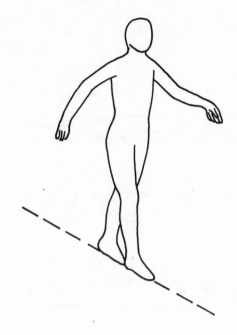

13. Angel Stretch

A   *Repeat 2 to 5 times*
B   *Repeat 5 times*
C   *Repeat 5 times*

Starting position: Lie on back, legs straight, feet together, arms extended at sides.

Action: *Count 1.* Move arms and legs outward along the floor to a spread-eagle position. Slide—do not raise—arms and legs. *Count 2.* Return to starting position.

Note: Throughout the exercise try to compress the lower back against the floor by tightening the abdominal muscles. Do not arch the lower back.

Value: Stretches muscles of arms, legs, trunk, aids posture; improves strength of abdominal muscles.

14. Walk a Straight Line

A   *only—walk for 10 feet*
B *and* **C**   *Skip this, do Walk the Beam (#15) instead.*

Starting position: Stand erect with left foot along a straight line. Arms held away from body to aid balance.

Action: *Count 1.* Walk the length of the straight line by putting the right foot in front of the left foot with right heel touching left toe, and then placing the feet alternately one in front of the other, heel-to-toe. *Count 2.* Return to the starting point by walking backward along the line, alternately placing one foot behind the other, toe-to-heel.

Value: Improves balance; helps posture.

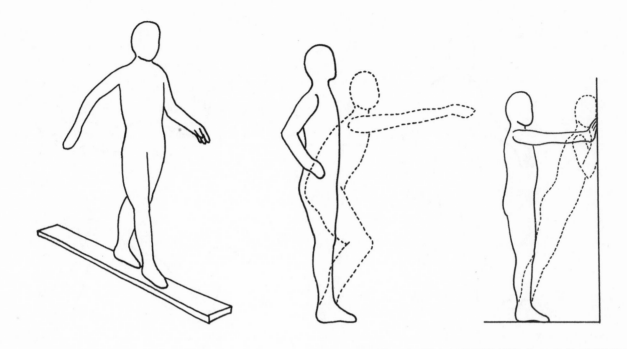

15. Walk the Beam

B *Walk 10 feet on 2" x 6" board*
C *Walk 10 feet on 2" x 4" board*

Starting position: Stand erect with left foot on board, long axis of foot in line with board.

Action: *Count 1.* Walk the length of the board by putting the right foot in front of the left foot with right heel touching left toe, and then placing the feet alternately one in front of the other, heel-to-toe. *Count 2.* Return to the starting point by walking backward along the length of the board, alternately placing one foot behind the other, toe-to-heel.

Note: The board is placed flat on the floor, not on the 2" edge.

Value: Improves balance; helps posture.

Note: *At this point in sequence*
A *perform Half Knee Bend (#8), repeating it 2 to 5 times; Wall Push-Away (#10) repeating 2 to 10 times; then skip #15, 16, & 17, moving to #18 next.*
B *Skip #16 and do #17 next.*

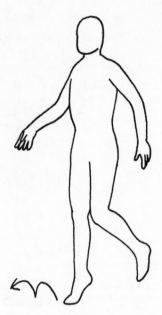

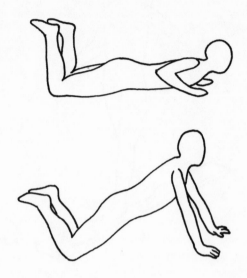

16. Hop

C   *Hop 5 times on each foot* **C** *only*

Starting position: Stand erect, weight on right foot, left leg bent slightly at the knee, and left foot held a few inches off the floor; arms held sideward slightly away from the body to aid balance.

Action: *Count 1.* Hop on right foot, moving few inches forward each hop.

Note: Perform the desired number of hops on right leg, then change to left leg and hop.

Value: Improves balance, strengthens extensor muscles of leg and foot; increases circulation.

17. Knee Push Up

B   *Repeat 1 to 3 times*
C   *Repeat 3 to 6 times*

Starting position: Lie on floor, face down, legs together, knees bent with feet raised off floor, hands on floor under shoulders, palms down.

Action: *Count 1.* Push upper body off floor until arms are fully extended and body is in straight line from head to knees. *Count 2.* Return to starting position.

Value: Strengthens muscles of arms, shoulders, and trunk.

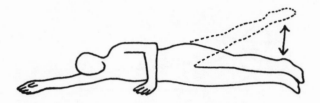 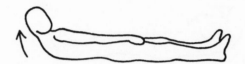

18. Side Leg Raise

A *Repeat 2 to 5 times each leg*
B *Repeat 5 to 10 times*
C *Repeat 10 times*

Starting position: Right side of body on floor, head resting on right arm. *Count 1.* Lift left leg sideward about 30 inches off floor. *Count 2.* Return to starting position.

Note: Do the desired number of repetitions with the left leg and then turn over, lie on left side and exercise the right leg.

Value: Helps improve flexibility of the hip joint and strengthens lateral muscles of trunk and hip.

19. Head and Shoulder Curl

A *Repeat 2 to 5 times;*
hold each for 4 seconds

Starting position: Lie on back, legs straight, feet together, arms extended along the front of the legs with palms resting lightly on the thighs.

Action: *Count 1.* Tighten abdominal muscles and lift head and shoulders so that shoulders are about 10 inches off the floor. Meanwhile slide arms along the legs, keeping them extended. Then hold the position for 4 seconds. *Count 2.* Return slowly to starting position, keeping abdominal muscles tight until shoulders and head rest on floor. Relax.

Note: A *skip Exercises #20, 21.*

19. Head and Shoulder Curl

B *Repeat 5 times;*
   hold each for 6 seconds

Same as A except on starting position arms are crossed over chest (kept in that position throughout).

Note: The head should lead in a "curling" motion, chin tucked to chest, back rounded, not arched.

Value: Excellent for improving abdominal strength and stretching back muscles.

19. Head and Shoulder Curl

C *Repeat 5 times;*
   hold each for 10 seconds

Same as A, except on starting position, hands are clasped behind the neck (held that way throughout).

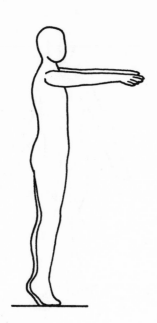

20. Diver's Stance

B *only*
Hold position for 10 seconds.

Starting position: Stand erect, feet slightly apart, arms at sides.

Action: Rise on toes and bring arms upward and forward so that they extend parallel with the floor, palms down. When this position is attained, close eyes and hold balance for 10 seconds.

Note: Head should be straight and body should be held firmly throughout.

Value: Improves balance; strengthens extensor muscles of feet and legs; helps maintain good posture.

21. Stork Stand

C *only*
Hold position 10 seconds on each leg.

Starting position: Stand erect, feet slightly apart, hands on hips, head straight.

Action: Transfer weight to the left foot and bend right knee, bringing the sole of the right foot to the inner side of the left knee. When this position is reached, close eyes and hold for 10 seconds.

Note: After holding on left leg, change to the right leg and repeat.

Value: Improves balance.

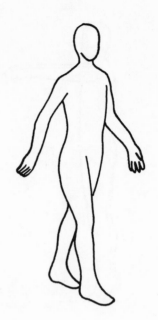

22. Alternate Walk-Jog

(Repeats Exercise #2)
A *Walk 50 steps, jog 10;
1 to 3 minutes.*
B *Walk 50 steps, jog 25;
3 to 6 minutes.*
C *Begin walk 50 steps, jog 50, gradually
increasing to walk 100 steps, jog 100;
continue for 5 minutes.*

Value: Provides an "interval" of exercise
for circulatory system, and for strength-
ening leg muscles.

23. Walk

(Repeats Exercise #1)
A *Walk 1 to 3 minutes*
B *Walk 1 to 3 minutes*
C *Walk 3 minutes*

Value: Tapering off, as heart rate, breathing, body heat, and other functions return
to normal.

Note: To order a copy of the booklet from
which this exercise program is taken, send
75¢ to
Superintendent of Documents
U.S. Government Printing Office
Washington, DC 20402
Ask for *The Fitness Challenge in the
Later Years,* stock number 017-062-00009-3.

CHAPTER 9

Food and Drugs

Nutrition

The basic nutrition needs of older people are not very different from those of any other adult, but several factors make it likely that you don't eat as well as you should. Some people who live alone do enjoy cooking for themselves; but most probably do not. It's easier to open a can or defrost a prepackaged dinner, but that is an expensive route to hidden malnutrition—which may be why you don't have as much energy as you wish you had. Still, you don't have to cook an elegant meal and dine at a pretty candle-lit table in order to eat well. It doesn't matter where or how you eat, it's what you eat that really counts. In this chapter you will find small ways to modify your diet that can pay off with a big improvement in energy, morale, and overall good health.

Food is our supply of energy and while this need tends to decrease with age, the decrease is perhaps less than we imagine. According to Dr. Jean Mayer in his book *A Diet for Living* the amount of calories we need "declines rapidly between the ages of 45 and 65, but relatively slowly from then to the age of 75, when it stabilizes."

In the 60s and 70s, Dr. Mayer says, you need one-third fewer calories than you did in your 20s, somewhat more if you exercise.

The significance, which can't be overstressed, of this need for a smaller total amount of food is that "every calorie must carry its weight in nutrients or deficiencies will occur." Mayer, along with virtually every other nutritionist, advises cutting down on sugar, fats, and bakery goods. It is essential, on the other hand, to keep up your consumption of milk (skim milk is fine), cheese, fish, poultry, whole cereals and grains, vegetables, and fruit.

Most of us, I expect, really don't know what we eat. For me, diet plans that talk in terms of grams of protein or portions of green and yellow vegetables sound so complicated that I give up before I begin. Judith Wurtman, of the Department of Nutrition and Food Science at Massachusetts Institute of Technology, suggests an easy first step in improving your diet. Dr. Wurtman advises that you keep a record of everything you eat for one whole week. Then look at it to see where the gaps are.

Here are some facts about the food you need and the food you eat, against which to check your week's food record.

Vitamins

Every natural food has vitamins, but some foods are better than others and different foods supply different vitamins. As my doctor always told me, you don't need vitamin pills if you eat a balanced diet. The trouble is that most older people do not eat a balanced diet, so a single multiple vitamin pill as a *supplement* to, not a replacement for, the natural vitamins you get from food may be a good idea. Massive doses of vitamins, however, can be harmful (even if they actually did what their proponents claim for them) and should never be taken except on a doctor's advice.

Vitamin E is currently being touted as the "anti-aging" vitamin. The case has by no means been proved and one researcher who believes vitamin E may have some anti-aging action also told me that there can be serious side effects in the excessive dosages prescribed by some proponents of this latter-day fountain of youth.

Older people, on the other hand, do need more vitamin C than they did when young. Vitamin C cannot be stored in the body and so must be eaten every day. Excellent sources of vitamin C are all citrus fruits, tomatoes, raw broccoli (delicious in salads), raw cabbage, red and green peppers (a surprisingly healthy vegetable, it turns out—*except* when covered with wax), and most dark green leafy vegetables. Of all fresh vitamin C sources, cabbage maintains the highest amount of it for the longest time. A whole orange not only has more vitamin C than juice, it also adds fiber to your diet. Vitamin C is perishable, so buy small cans of frozen juice and use fresh vegetables as quickly as possible.

Vegetables

Raw vegetables are more nutritious than cooked ones and overcooked vegetables aren't much good at all. Try to eat at least one third of your vegetables in a salad. Cook vegetables in the smallest possible amount of water—an inexpensive steamer that fits in any pot is a good way to get crisp, healthy veggies.

When you buy vegetables, select the darkest ones you can. The deeper the color, the greater the concentration of nutrients. Choose spinach or dark-leaved greens instead of iceberg lettuce, which doesn't offer much but crunch. Sweet potatoes, squash, carrots, yellow turnips instead of white—all of these are extremely high in vitamin A.

Can Diet Improve Memory?

The brain has long been thought to be an organ above all others in the body to the extent that its needs for oxygen and nutrients are always met first. Thus, under normal circumstances, the amount of certain substances circulating in the blood at any time would not have an effect upon the brain, since if they were in short supply, the brain would automatically have first call on whatever it required.

Recent work by Dr. Richard J. Wurtman and his colleagues in the Department of Nutrition and Food Science at M.I.T. makes this view of the brain "as an autonomous organ, largely independent of metabolic processes, no longer tenable." Wurtman and his associates have found that each meal, depending upon its composition, can directly alter the levels of certain substances in the brain.

The possible significance of this for memory improvement lies in the ability to raise the level of choline in the brain through increasing the amount of lecithin in the diet. Choline, the active ingredient in lecithin, is a compound found in vitamin B complex. It produces a neurotransmitter, a chemical needed to send nerve impulses. Higher levels of choline increase these transmissions, which has led some researchers to conclude that learning ability and memory can be improved through increasing one's intake of lecithin.

In one study, subjects given an injection of choline chloride before the test, improved by 20 percent their ability to memorize a series of words. Dr. Wurtman has found that when choline is provided in the form of lecithin, it has an even greater effect than in its pure state.

Lecithin is a natural food substance found in its highest concentration in soybean oil and to a lesser extent in corn oil and other vegetable oils. In capsule or powder form, it can be found in health food stores and drug stores. As a dietary supplement, one teaspoon, or five grams, is the usual recommended amount.

Eggs

Eggs are good for you because they are high in protein and bad for you because they are high in cholesterol. Fortunately, the egg is divisible into two parts and it is possible to eat eggs in such a way as to get all of the good and none of the bad.

All the cholesterol in the egg is in the yolk and most of the protein (*lots* of it) is in the white. Make scrambled eggs from three whites and one yolk, or fry them the same way. Give the extra yolks to your cat or dog or throw them away. This may be the hardest part of an otherwise easy operation since it appears to be wasting food. Think of the extra yolks as you do an orange peel or steak bone, or even the eggshell—in other words, an inedible part—and you'll soon get used to it. Eggs are a cheap source of protein in its most usable form for the body.

Sugar

Sugar is aptly called "empty calories" because it contains no protein, no vitamins, and no minerals. More than that, it forms acids that deplete the body's source of calcium and it destroys important B vitamins. If you managed to cut out every bit of added sugar, you'd still be eating sugar in practically every processed food you bought, from canned soup to cold cereals.

But even if you can't eliminate all the sugar, it is possible to cut down on it. Eat fresh fruit instead of canned. When you buy canned fruit, choose the one with the label that says "packed in its own juice" instead of heavy (or even light) syrup. Make applesauce with cinnamon instead of sugar; it keeps well in the refrigerator and can be frozen in small quantities—in the long run, fresh fruit is easier to carry home from the store than jars, certainly cheaper, and much healthier. If you must add a sweetener to foods, try honey, which has some nutrients.

Bread, Cake, and Other Starches

White flour is a nutritional disaster. Enriched white flour isn't much better. In the process of refining the flour, a multitude of nutrients are removed—*enriched* means that a *few* of them have been put back. If a bread has to be described as enriched, you can be sure it isn't rich in food nutrients. Also, having removed the natural bran from wheat flour during the refining process, now that we are belatedly realizing the need for this fiber in our diets, we find it replaced as an additive.

Buy 100 percent whole grain bread (some so-called whole wheat bread is also partly white flour); sprinkle wheat germ, which you can buy in any supermarket, on cereal, yogurt, and cottage cheese, and add it to hamburgers. Eat bran muffins instead of sweet rolls; brown rice instead of white, and whole wheat pastas if you can find them.

Protein

One of the many reasons that eating sugar and starches isn't good for you is that they fill you up without supplying needed protein. As Dr. Mayer said, when you eat fewer calories, you have to make them all count or you will be full but malnourished. Eggs, meat, fish, and poultry are the main sources of complete proteins. Red meat, which is high in cholesterol, isn't as high in protein as poultry or fish. Other sources of protein are nuts, beans, and milk products.

Dairy Foods

Milk and cheese are excellent sources of protein and calcium. Older people—contrary to the myth that says calcium is for growing children—have a very real need for this mineral. Two glasses of milk a day should be your minimum. Make it skim milk to cut down on the fat if you can. If you want to make it taste richer and also increase the amount of protein and calcium, add dry skim milk to the liquid.

Cottage cheese is an excellent source of protein. So is any natural cheese. Avoid processed cheeses, especially in jars, since they have about as much coloring, preservatives, artificial flavors, and filler material as they have cheese.

Snacks, Substitutes, and Healthy Additives

An excellent between meals or bedtime snack is a glass of milk accompanied by peanut butter on whole wheat crackers. Most supermarkets now sell natural peanut butter (make sure no sugar has been added), which is the only kind to eat. Processed peanut butter is high in saturated fats and preservatives. Peanut butter plus a milk product makes a complete protein.

Yogurt may or may not be an anti-aging food, but it is as healthy as it can be and as easy to prepare as opening the container. Use it as a substitute for sour cream; or for dessert over sliced fruit, especially bananas, which are themselves one of the most nutritious of foods. Try sliced bananas with coffee yogurt.

Instead of candies, nibble on cashews or peanuts. These two nuts are higher than most in protein and lower in saturated fats. Roasted soybeans or sunflower seeds are even better. Dried fruits will satisfy your sweet tooth and supply important minerals. Fresh fruit is a perfect snack.

A protein-rich breakfast is important at any age. A juice-coffee-toast-with-jam breakfast causes a rapid rise in your blood-sugar level with an accompanying sudden and severe drop. Protein for breakfast keeps the blood-sugar level higher and steadier for a longer time; when it drops, it doesn't drop to such a low level. If you can't give up your toast, make it 100 percent whole wheat toast. Instead of cream cheese and jam, use cottage cheese, natural hard cheese, or peanut butter on the bread.

Medications

Americans over 65 comprise 10 percent of the population, yet buy a staggering 25 percent of all prescription drugs. These drugs often cause paradoxical or adverse reactions in older people. While pharmacologists know that infants and young children require special dosages, medications for old people are prescribed in much the same manner as they are for young adults—even though, with age, drug metabolism is not as effective and a general lower body metabolism prolongs the action of a drug.

Writing of what he calls "iatrogenic (doctor-induced) disorders," Dr. Robert N. Butler, Director of the National Institute on Aging, says that drugs are given far too readily, without adequate consideration of possible long- or short-term side effects, which can be extremely serious or even fatal.

Twelve of the twenty most commonly prescribed drugs for people over 65 have a sedating effect, which can result in impairment of physical speed and coordination. A side effect to *that* side effect is fear and depression on the part of the patient, who quite naturally equates this slowing down to age and/or illness, rather than to the medication. Although depression is often treated with drugs, depression in older people is often caused by drugs.

"Judicious use of drugs for ailments of old age can be enormously helpful," says Dr. Butler, "but it must be emphasized that many drugs tend to reinforce the normal slowing down of responses and the sense of aging and depression."

Overmedication, especially with tranquilizers, is "one of the commonest causes of blunting and confusion in older people," says gerontologist Alex Comfort. He advises that you should always tell your doctor what pills you are taking, even if he is the one who prescribed them. "Doctors, too, can be forgetful."

Some drugs, in addition to causing unexpected reactions, alone or in combination with other medications, have a long half life. Twenty-four hours after you take Valium, at least half the drug is still in your system. If you take Valium to go to sleep and then take it or another pill the next day, the original Valium will escalate the reaction.

Dr. John Rowe, chief of gerontology at Beth Israel Hospital in Boston, calls the mixing of drugs extremely dangerous. "When you need several doctors for different ailments, each doctor gives you a prescription without knowing what the other prescribed. This can produce drug-induced illnesses, which are a major concern today." Obviously, a doctor ought to ask what pills you are taking, but if he doesn't, tell him.

Dr. Rowe also warns against hoarding pills. "Medicines change over a long period of time, just as people do." He suggests putting all your old pills into a brown bag and taking them to the doctor to see which should be thrown out. You should also note the expiration date on the bottles and get rid of outdated medicines.

Alcohol

Drinking can become a serious problem for older people, even for those who never had any trouble with it before. This is partly because of decreasing tolerance, partly because of alcohol's incompatability with other drugs (of which older people take probably too many), and partly, in Alex Comfort's words, "because society makes age so stressful that people drink to escape it."

Dr. Robert Butler calls alcohol a "big" cause of senility. "We are beginning to see a shocking amount of excessive alcohol intake ... in people who never drank in their lives. Many are older women who may start to drink to forget their loneliness, to overcome the pain from arthritis, to deal with grief of one sort or another."

"For people who are lonely, sick, or have life problems," says Dr. Comfort, "alcohol is a far more dangerous drug than heroin because it's around and all your well-meaning friends are pushers."

CHAPTER 10

Our Future Selves: New Directions in Research on Aging

Research in the field of aging is not, of course, brand new, but it was not until 1975, with the formation of the National Institute on Aging, that it was given status and a new sense of direction. Where previous emphasis was on the disabilities of old age—now beginning to be seen as sometimes due to social, rather than purely medical, adversities—the National Institute on Aging supports the concept that "the study of aging is not just an examination of decline, loss, and decrement. Rather, it is an exploration of the normal processes of development that are fundamental to life and continue into old age, and about which we know too little."

These processes, writes Dr. Robert N. Butler, Director of the NIA, "include creativity, life experience, perspective, and judgment. Indeed, the overall objective of NIA research is to examine the variety of factors—biological, psychological, and social—which constitute the aging process, and translate this knowledge into ways of preventing, promoting, modifying, or reversing these factors so that life is better and more dignified in the later years."

Research on aging may be divided into two general areas. One is the disease processes that characterize old age. The other is the aging process itself, and the biomedical, behavioral, and societal changes that comprise it. The diseases of old age have been, and still are, the subject of research attention from the various components of the National Institutes of Health. The biomedical, behavioral, and social aspects of aging are the concern of the National Institute on Aging.*

* The material in this chapter is adapted from an article by Dr. Butler, describing the research programs of the National Institute on Aging, in *Public Health Reports,* and from the booklet, *Our Future Selves,* prepared by the NIA and published by the Department of Health, Education and Welfare.

Dr. Robert N. Butler, who won the Pulitzer Prize for his book, *Why Survive? Being Old in America,* is director of the National Institute on Aging, the newest and smallest division of the National Institutes of Health.

Biomedical Aspects of Aging

Basic and clinical biomedical research can improve the quality of life for the aged by relieving many of their painful disabilities, enable more people fully to realize their natural life span, and guide the creation of effective health services.

To approach these goals, we must be able to distinguish aging from disease. The elderly ill—and usually their families and doctors—commonly attribute many of their symptoms to aging, and therefore consider them immutable, when in fact the illnesses may be treatable. Cancer and stroke, painful and crippled joints, mental confusion, and heart disease are not the inevitable tolls of aging; rather, they are the results of a variety of causes not intrinsically related to age. On the other hand, normal physiological changes of aging should not be regarded as diagnostic signs of diseases such as hypertension and diabetes.

But aging *is* the result of a series of fundamental, if poorly understood, biological changes. For example, normal changes in the immune system with age determine a person's resistance to infection. Decreased immune response is probably a major factor in the apparent increased susceptibility of the elderly to infectious diseases.

As one of the most exciting and promising fields in biomedical research today, immunology holds a key to improving the health of people of all ages. An NIA grantee at the University of California in Los Angeles placed mice on diets moderately restricted in calories or proteins and not only increased resistance to some viral infections and certain tumors, but also prolonged their life span. Evidently, the immune systems of the mice stayed "younger" on these special diets.

Immunology may also play a major role in senile dementia. Autoimmunity, in which the immune response attacks tissues in one's own body, has been theorized to be one cause of senile dementia. "Senility" is a lay term that is medically known as organic brain syndrome. There may be as many as a hundred causes of senility. When the underlying cause is recognized and treated, there is an excellent chance of reversing the state.

Better treatment for the elderly is essential to improving the quality of later years, but many factors are involved. Too often today, the physician and family settle for an incomplete diagnosis or course of therapy because the person is old and must expect to be ill. (An elderly volunteer in the National Institute of Health's Human Aging Study, from 1955–1966, went to the doctor about a pain in his left leg. The doctor declared, "Sam, for Pete's sake, what do you expect at 102?" Sam retorted, "My right leg is also 102 and it doesn't hurt a bit. How do you explain that?")

Improved diagnosis and treatment depend, however, on more extensive knowledge about the aging body — what is normal for it and how, for example, it reacts to drugs. Older Americans use about 25 percent of all prescription drugs, although they represent only 10 percent of the population, and, in fact, drugs constitute the largest medical expenditure older people must meet almost entirely on their own.

Medications are prescribed for the elderly in much the same manner as they are for younger adults, although the effects are often not the same. More research is essential to determine optimal doses and to define possible toxic, as well as long- or short-term side effects.

Behavioral Aspects of Aging

The elderly are a diverse group, with individual differences more telling than their similarities. But to aid analysis, the aged population can be divided into the old and very old. The old are those as young as 60, probably retired, usually healthy and vigorous, often anxious to apply their talents, knowledge, and time meaningfully, and therefore constituting a valuable if often unused resource. The very old are 75 or older. Many in this group are vigorous and self-sufficient; others can manage their lives if given some support by health and social services; a small number, but one that increases with age, need sustained support.

Even allowing for this division of the aged into two groups, they still remain a highly diverse population, not readily quantified or labeled. Also, there are not adequate theories to help us understand the behavior of aging persons or groups. That is true whether the pertinent discipline is pyschology, sociology, anthropology, economics, or political science. However, research that began in the 1950s has led to several insights on which future research programs can be based.

One such insight—in contrast to the prevailing myths—is that most normal older people are intellectually and socially able, productive (given the opportunity), mentally vigorous, interested in their surroundings, eager to participate in the social life of family, kin, and community. Where there are decrements and apparent declines, the cause is not necessarily the biological process of aging, but often controllable impositions only partially related to age—disease, social isolation, poor diet, limited education, economic plight. This view forces the conclusion that it is possible to prevent or treat many of the intellectual, social, and emotional problems of a significant number of the aged population. Moreover, it emphasizes the ability of many of the aged, given the opportunity, to lead independent, self-sustaining, satisfying lives.

This is supported by the demonstrable fact that integration of the older person in the society is the norm, rather than the exception, in every society that has been carefully studied, including the United States. Institutionalization is limited to a tiny fraction of the aged.

On the other hand, people over 65 commit 25 percent of the suicides in the United States. Obviously, therefore, the golden years appear quite tarnished to many. Gerontologists need a better understanding of the psychological changes and problems of older people.

Mandatory retirement is a common practice in this country. This, coupled with the unwillingness of many companies to hire people who are in late middle age, means that a large segment of the population is forced into retirement or jobs requiring less skill than they possess. Since mandatory retirement may well be declared unconstitutional in the future, we must be able to assess who is ready for retirement and who is not, based on such factors as competence, economic needs, and

Keep Warm

If you are over 65, keep the temperature up to 65°F. And if you are over 75, keep it over 70°F. Leave energy conservation to somebody else.

That warning, issued during the bitterly cold winter of 1978 by the National Institute on Aging, is based on a little known but serious condition called Accidental Hypothermia.

While everyone's health is endangered by lengthy exposure to very cold temperatures, the old are particularly vulnerable. Even mildly cool temperatures of 60 to 65°F can trigger accidental hypothermia, a drop in deep body temperature that can be fatal if not detected and treated properly. (A drop in *skin* temperature, which happens frequently, is not hypothermia because it doesn't necessarily reflect the *internal* body temperature.) Diseases of the veins and arteries and treatment with certain drugs make a person more susceptible.

The elderly probably account for nearly half of all victims of accidental hypothermia. Infants under 1 year old are also susceptible. So, for unknown reasons, are some adults between 35 and 64. Among the elderly, the likeliest victims are the very old, the poor who are unable to afford adequate heating, and those whose bodies do not respond to cold normally. The greatest risk is to the aged whose body temperature regulation is defective; they do not shiver and therefore cannot conserve body heat when they need it most. Most victims of accidental hypothermia do not shiver. While others are putting on sweaters, they may insist they are comfortable.

How to protect yourself?

All older people, but especially those over 75, should avoid prolonged exposure to even *mild* cold without taking care to keep warm. In addition to keeping your home temperature at 70°F or more, you should wear adequate clothing, including sweaters, robes, a hat or cap, and thick socks. Have enough blankets on your bed.

If you are taking medication to treat anxiety, depressions, nervousness, or nausea, check with your doctor to determine whether the drug is a phenothiazine. Since these drugs can impair the body's response to cold, the physician may want to use a different medication.

personal desires. The NIA is interested in the effects of mandatory retirement and in developing effective retirement test patterns.

Social Aspects of Aging

Why do young people fear old age? What effect will the growing elderly segment of our population have on our society? Does aging differ in various groups in our country?

We need research to determine the reason for ageism, the negative attitude toward aging held by much of our society. Improving the physical and mental health and the economic well-being of our older citizens will do much to enhance the attitudes of the rest of society toward aging.

There are rather significant differences in life expectancies for some subgroups in our society. Blacks, Mexican-Americans, and American Indians have noticeably shorter life expectancies than whites, probably because of socioeconomic disadvantages. Many of these people cannot expect to live long enough to benefit from social security and Medicare. Besides taking steps to improve the life expectancies for future generations, we should take measures now to enable more elderly people from minority groups to share the benefits available to white Americans after the age of 65.

Baltimore Study of Aging

Psychological and social factors of aging, as well as the biological aspects, are under evaluation in the Baltimore Longitudinal Study of Aging. Since 1958, this study has periodically examined 650 men to monitor cardiac, renal, and pulmonary function, body composition, exercise, physiology, carbohydrate and lipid metabolism, drug pharmokinetics, nutrition and endocrine factors; and behavioral and social variables. Already data from this longitudinal study suggest that exercise may lead to a longer life. In 1977, NIA prepared to add women to the study to make it more valid and comprehensive for the whole population.

Shortage of Researchers

Basic to all future research on aging is an adequate supply of trained investigators. Gerontology and geriatric medicine are simply not recognized by many people in the scientific and medical worlds. Thus, there is a shortage of trained manpower now and few people to interest young investigators in the field. Furthermore, scientists who are beginning their careers in gerontology often have difficulty in funding their projects. Established researchers in other fields who may wish to change the direction of their studies to aging research are unable to get support necessary for their training. The NIA is taking steps in several areas to help overcome the obstacles to the development of a trained cadre of investigators.

Repeatedly, we hear that Americans value things, including people, according to their productive capacity. The elderly—as a group—are thus viewed as burdens. Yet, they can and do contribute much, given the chance. To increase their opportunities for more meaningful later years, research on aging has shifted from its exclusive disease orientation toward a more comprehensive investigation of the normal physiological changes with age, the behavioral constitution of the aged, and the social, cultural, and economic environment in which the elderly live. This is the direction that present and future research on aging must take so that the increasing numbers of older people, realizing their full capacities, will be valued and respected by any standard.

Part IV

Institutions, Organizations, and Agencies

CHAPTER 11

College Gerontology Programs

The study of gerontology and preparation for careers in the field of aging may represent the educational baby boom of the late seventies and early eighties. Unlike geriatric medicine, which is still woefully lagging behind the times, gerontology programs are springing up in colleges at a remarkable rate.

The field of gerontology is to a large extent interdisciplinary; that is, it can combine studies in sociology, psychology, social work, education, medicine, biology, physiology, home economics, anthropology, theology, public administration, and hospital administration.

Similarly, the jobs that this career training leads to are correspondingly varied: professionals and paraprofessionals may work in public and private agencies; hospitals; nursing homes; community programs for recreation, counseling, housing, and nutrition; and university and other research programs.

New emphases in gerontology include such areas as nursing home administration, community development, social work, psychology, and architecture.

While the study of gerontology is a new subject for students beginning their academic life, it is also a popular one for people already working in the field and for many looking for a late-life career. And a lot of older people are studying gerontology whether or not they see it as a career. To accommodate those already at work in the field, many colleges offer gerontology courses in the late afternoon or early evening.

Most, although not all, of the colleges in this selected list are members of the Association for Gerontology in Higher Education. However, many colleges that *are* members of the Association are not included here because their programs are still in the planning stages. By the time you read this, a book describing the programs and planned programs of the 125 members of the Association will be available. For information, write:

The Association for Gerontology in Higher Education
1 DuPont Circle, N.W.
Washington, DC 20036

Space limitations have dictated certain omissions in the listings in this chapter. In addition to ignoring programs planned for the future, I have not listed those offered by two-year community colleges. By all means, check with those colleges in your area, since many of them offer courses in gerontology. Space also forbids anything but the very briefest description of a program, since you will obviously write for full details from the colleges that interest you.

Alabama
University of Alabama
Center for the Study of Aging
University, AL 35486
Dr. Lorin A. Baumhover, Director

The Center for the Study of Aging was established in 1972 to provide leadership in education, research, and service in the field of aging.

The center offers a graduate Specialist in Gerontology Certificate program and coordinates gerontology course offerings of the various departments and divisions of the university. In addition, the center sponsors numerous conferences, workshops, and short-term training events in aging.

California
University of California at San Francisco
Human Development and Aging Program
Langley Porter Institute
San Francisco, CA 94143
Marjorie Fiske, Director

This is the major training program in aging for the University of California's graduate students enrolled in other behavioral science programs, who are interested in specializing in human development. Offers a Ph.D. in human development and aging.

University of California at Berkeley
School of Social Work
Berkeley, CA 94720
Mary O'Day, Chairperson, Gerontology Studies

Offers Master of Social Welfare degree with specialty in gerontology and Doctor of Social Welfare degree with emphasis in gerontology.

San Francisco State University
1600 Holloway Avenue
San Francisco, CA 94132
Anabel O. Pelham, Coordinator

The Applied Gerontology Certificate Program is designed primarily for persons working or planning to work in the field of aging. The curriculum varies and provides practical information useful to applied health personnel, community service personnel, clergy, educators, program directors and administrators, pre-retirement planners and counselors, and urban planners.

Courses are offered in the evening and occasionally are held off campus. Weekend workshops are offered throughout each term.

University of Southern California

Ethel Percy Andrus Gerontology Center
University Park
Los Angeles, CA 90007
James E. Birren, Director

One of the most important, comprehensive gerontology centers in the country. The focus of the center is unique in that its thrust includes both the biological and behavioral aspects of aging. The operations are divided into four principal areas: The Research Institute, composed of seven laboratories; the Leonard Davis School of Gerontology, offering bachelor's and master's degrees; Educational Development, offering short-term training in aging throughout the year; and Community Programs, which extends the center's research and training efforts to the Los Angeles community. The center has an extensive research library and publishes monographs and technical bibliographies.

California State College at Dominguez Hills

Dominguez Hills, CA 90747
Antonia M. Bercovici, Director, Human
Services Program

Students can major in gerontology as undergraduates and at the master's degree level. An annual Summer Institute in Gerontology is geared for both people working in the field and for those planning their own retirements. Students may complete the entire thirty-two units required for a certificate in gerontology in one summer or over several summer sessions.

California State University

Fresno, CA 93740

California State University offers a multidisciplinary minor in gerontology that requires fourteen semester units in basic and core courses with full gerontology content. Part of this requirement is fulfilled by participation in a "friendly visitor" program

with the aging. A total of twenty-one to twenty-four semester units is required.

The minor is designed to serve undergraduate students in any major, but especially for those majoring in communicative disorders, health science, home economics, physical therapy, psychology, recreation, social welfare, and sociology.

San Diego State University

University Center for Gerontology
San Diego, CA 92101
E. Percil Stanford, Director

A multidisciplinary program with emphasis in sociology, psychology, nursing, health science and safety, social work, recreation, family studies and consumer science, and biology.

San Jose State University

Gerontology Training and Education
Center
San Jose, CA 95192
Lu Charlotte, Director

San Jose State University offers an undergraduate minor in gerontology, which uses an interdisciplinary and intergenerational approach. The program also includes field experience. An interdepartmental certificate program in applied gerontology is also offered, aimed at professionals and paraprofessionals in the field. Persons seeking an introductory core curriculum for career possibilities may also enter this program. Older students are eligible for the "over-60" fee-waiver program.

Connecticut
University of Connecticut

Human Development Center
Storrs, CT 06268
Howard A. Rosencranz, Director

The University of Connecticut received a grant in 1976 from the Department of Health, Education and Welfare's Administration on Aging for support of the Human Development Center. The center publishes a newsletter and coordinates academic programs. Degree training in gerontology is available in eight academic areas. Short-term, nondegree offerings in aging are available through the Division of Continuing Education.

University of Bridgeport
Center for the Study of Aging
Bridgeport, CT 06602
David K. Carboni, Chairman

Full-time and part-time students, as well as transfer students, may enter the gerontology undergraduate programs. Academic programs are designed for recent high-school graduates as well as paraprofessionals and professionals currently employed in the field. The center suggests that the study of gerontology is also appropriate for college graduates who wish to earn a second degree, for the individual who may be changing careers, and as enrichment studies for elderly persons.

Financial aid to students and special tuition rates for qualified older persons are available. Also, the university offers a tuition-free program to persons over 62 years of age.

With the advice of the Center for the Study of Aging, the university's colleges, community agencies, and older persons are developing a range of cultural, professional, and experimental activities to meet the needs of the older community.

District of Columbia
University of the District of Columbia
Institute of Gerontology
425 Second Street, N.W.
Washington, DC 20001
Clavin Fields, Director

Graduate and undergraduate gerontology core courses offered, scheduled in late afternoon, evenings, and on Saturdays to accommodate students with full-time jobs. Internships in selected gerontological settings are required of all students. Special courses for older adults are offered at no charge.

Florida
University of Florida
Center for Gerontological Studies and Programs
Gainesville, FL 32611
Carter C. Osterbind, Director

The Center for Gerontological Studies and Programs was established in 1971 to plan and develop a broad multidisciplinary involvement of the university in the field of aging. At this point, it provides an organization through which faculty members from many disciplines may work to study problems of aging, develop programs of benefit to the aged, provide career-related experiences for graduate and professional students, and disseminate research information.

Graduate and professional students in advanced degree programs may concentrate in gerontology. When fully developed, the program will cover undergraduate education, too, as well as programs in continuing education, research, and public service.

Florida State University
Institute for Social Research
Multidisciplinary Center on Gerontology
Tallahassee, FL 32306
William G. Bell, Director

The Multidisciplinary Center on Gerontology was established with the aid of a grant from the U.S. Administration on Aging, and has as its goals the training of individuals for careers in gerontology; additional training for those already in the field; research; and community service.

The program of studies in gerontology is not a degree program. Rather, students earn a graduate degree in their host department with an emphasis in gerontology. Participating host departments are social work, home and family life, education management systems, and urban and regional planning. The center will work with any student showing an interest in gerontology, regardless of departmental affiliation.

Courses are complemented by an internship, enabling students to gain actual work experience.

The center also sponsors a series of colloquia, in which prominent professionals in the field make presentations in an informal atmosphere; the Multidisciplinary Seminar on Gerontology; short courses; and workshops and conferences.

A small number of stipends is available from the center for graduate study in departments participating in the program for gerontological study.

University of Miami

Institute for the Study of Aging
1217A Dickinson Dr.
Coral Gables, FL 33124
Yvonne L. Leber, Staff Coordinator

The University of Miami has developed a certificate program for graduate students who wish to concentrate in aging studies. The Institute for the Study of Aging also oversees research and community service programs, including workshops and symposia. These conferences have attracted more than a thousand people and have dealt with such topics as "Communication Problems of the Aging" and "The Older Woman in Society."

University of South Florida

College of Social and Behavioral
Sciences
Aging Studies Program
Tampa, FL 33620
Wiley P. Mangum, Associate Professor of
Gerontology

The primary objective of the graduate program in aging is to train personnel for leadership positions in the planning, development, delivery, and evaluation of community services for older persons. In keeping with this objective, the program offers a broad range of cross-disciplinary courses. As an important part of the training process, each graduate spends a supervised internship for one academic quarter in a community agency or facility that provides

services for older persons. A master of arts degree in gerontology is awarded upon satisfactory completion of the requirements.

Georgia

Georgia State University

Gerontology Center
University Plaza
Atlanta, GA 30303
Barbara P. Payne, Director

In July 1978 the Gerontology Center added undergraduate courses in gerontology to its graduate programs. It also offers certificate programs to both graduate and nondegree students.

University of Georgia

Faculty on Gerontology
Athens, GA 30602
James E. Montgomery, Chairman

The University of Georgia offers a great many noncredit conferences and short courses related to aging.

Hawaii

University of Hawaii at Manoa

School of Public Health—School of
Social Work
Honolulu, HI 96822
Anthony Lenzer, Director, Gerontology
Training Program

Offers master's degrees in public health and in social work with specialization in gerontology. The university also grants a Bachelor of Science degree in human development, with a life cycle focus. Part-time students may enroll in the public health program. Hawaii residents over 60 are entitled to free tuition.

Illinois

University of Chicago

Adult Development and Aging Program
Committee on Human Development
5730 S. Woodlawn Avenue
Chicago, IL 60637
Bernice L. Neugarten, Director

The major emphasis is on preparation for a scholarly career in the area of life-span psychology and in social and psychological aspects of aging. Emphasis is on the preparation of researchers and teachers. A small number of students are given special training for research in mental health in the second half of life (a special program carried out in collaboration with the Department of Psychiatry at Northwestern University). These programs lead only to the Ph.D. The School of Social Service Administration also has a program in aging that trains professionals in service provision and in policy issues, and leads to both M.A. and Ph.D. degrees. Students may also concentrate in the economics of aging.

Students participate with faculty in a wide range of research projects—on adult sex roles, life transitions and the use of family, self-help groups, and other community support systems, personality patterns in middle-aged and older persons of different ethnic groups, forms of leisure and play in different age groups, productivity in persons over 60, aging and political ideology, memory and depression in the aged, systems of mental health care of older people, and evaluation of service programs for older people.

University of Illinois
    1901 University Hall, Box 4348
    Chicago, IL 60680
    Thomas O. Byerts, Director of
        Gerontology

The University of Illinois has an all-university committee on gerontology with membership from the three campuses, Chicago Circle, Medical Center, and Urbana-Champaign. The goal is to develop a strong interdisciplinary program of research, education, and service in aging.

Southern Illinois University
    Gerontology Program
    Edwardsville, IL 62026
    Dr. Anthony J. Traxler, Director

The Gerontology Program provides educational and training opportunities in aging to undergraduate and graduate students from various disciplines and professional programs throughout the university, as well as to professionals and paraprofessionals in the community who are currently providing services to the elderly. Direct service programs to the aging and research on various aspects of aging are also an integral part of the program. Graduate level training includes an interdisciplinary graduate specialization in gerontology. Students completing the gerontology specialization are awarded a certificate.

Indiana
Ball State University
    Institute of Gerontology
    Muncie, IN 47306
    H. Mason Atwood, Director

The Institute of Gerontology administers interdisciplinary academic programs in gerontology including: a master of arts degree with a major in applied gerontology; a doctoral cognate in applied gerontology; a graduate minor (master's degree level) in gerontology; and an undergraduate minor in gerontology.

The institute offers noncredit as well as credit programs in gerontology including: the Kirkpatrick Memorial Workshop on Aging, a one-day workshop that attracts some 500 participants annually; retirement planning seminars; Teacher Education Program on Aging; and various workshops and conferences.

The institute provides consultant and planning services to communities, agencies, and institutions in Indiana.

Kansas
Wichita State University
    University Gerontology Center
    Wichita, KS 67208
    Dr. William C. Hays, Acting Director

Because gerontology is concerned with gaining and applying knowledge about all aspects of aging in a wide range of profes-

Geriatric Medicine

While gerontology, the study of aging, is a booming discipline in the academic community, the same cannot be said for geriatric medicine. At the present time, according to Dr. Robert Butler, Director of the National Institute on Aging, only forty-four of the 120 U.S. medical schools offer any electives in geriatrics. Not a single school requires systematic training of all its students in long-term facilities and home-care programs.

In early 1977, the first endowed chair of geriatric medicine was set up at the New York Hospital-Cornell Medical Center, but in spite of the best efforts of the school, the chair was still unfilled a year and a half later.

Moreover, says Dr. Butler, physicians and medical students share the "dominant cultural value of ageism, which is particularly disturbing in light of the critical role played by the medical profession in the lives of the elderly."

sional settings, both the graduate and undergraduate programs at Wichita State are multidisciplinary. The center also acts as a resource center and information clearinghouse to assist community agencies and organizations in planning and developing services for older people.

Kansas State University
   Center for Aging
   Manhattan, KS 66506
   Marla L. Berg, Training Outreach
      Coordinator

The center is developing a multidisciplinary training program at both the graduate and undergraduate levels. The graduate program is expected to be implemented by the academic year 1979–1980.

Kentucky
University of Kentucky Medical Center
   Sanders-Brown Research Center on
      Aging
   Lexington, KY 40508
   Marcia M. Blacker, Staff Associate

The center has developed multidisciplinary programs concerned with the development of research knowledge, teaching, and service in the areas of gerontology. Its focus includes both the biology of aging and the development of programs dealing with the improvement of the quality of life. The center recognizes the need for service to the community and has available twenty-five public-service messages on topics of interest to the aging, which are aired by several local radio stations each day. Plans are underway for television programming.

Maryland
University of Maryland
   Center on Aging
   College Park, MD 20742
   Judy Olsen, Director

Courses on aging are offered in many departments, with new courses added every year. A certificate in aging is offered at the bachelor's, master's, and doctoral levels. The center also conducts research projects.

Massachusetts

Brandeis University

Florence Heller Graduate School of
Social Welfare
Waltham, MA 02154
Robert Binstock, Director, Program in
the Economics and Politics of Aging

This advanced degree program focuses
primarily on the economic, political, and
programmatic contexts of aging, such as:
public and private income maintenance
programs; industrial gerontology; the current and future economic status of the
aged; political attitudes and behavior of aging persons and age-based organizations;
and evaluation and impact research on policies and programs that affect the aging.

Boston University

Gerontology Center
730 Commonwealth Avenue
Boston, MA 02215
Louis Lowy and F. Marott Sinex,
Directors

The Boston University School of Social
Work offers a master's degree in direct
service practice or in administration/man-
agement, with a gerontology concentration.
The administration/management concentration is made possible by a grant received
by the Boston University Gerontology Center through a consortium for training
formed with Brandeis University.

The University's Metropolitan College
has several graduate and undergraduate
courses in gerontology. The School of
Nursing offers the opportunity to pursue
an interest in gerontology within the master's program in community health nursing.

The Graduate School permits a small
number of students to work out programs
of interdisciplinary studies that combine
work within two or more departments,
leading to the Ph.D. degree.

Michigan

University of Michigan

Institute of Gerontology

520 E. Liberty
Ann Arbor, MI 48109
Harold R. Johnson, Co-Director

The Specialist in Aging certificate is
awarded in conjunction with a graduate degree at the university. If a student already
holds a master's or doctoral degree, he or
she may pursue the certificate independently. The certificate may also be earned
through the Continuing Education program by submitting verification of an
earned graduate degree. Field work or research internship is required of all students.

In addition to the degree programs, the
institute has an extensive continuing education program that offers opportunities
for professionals to upgrade skills and
knowledge in the field of gerontology. It
also provides a means by which persons interested in midlife career changes can enter
the field of gerontology through enrollment
in a series of short-term seminars. The institute offers a wide variety of seminars,
workshops, and conferences.

University of Michigan tuition, for those
enrolled for credit, and Continuing Education tuition, for seminars and workshops,
can be reduced for students over 65.

The institute also conducts programs at,
and has a cooperative arrangement with,
Wayne State University in Detroit.

Wayne State University

Institute of Gerontology
Detroit, MI 48202
Charles J. Parrish, Co-director

The Institute of Gerontology is a joint
organization of the University of Michigan
and Wayne State.
See University of Michigan, above.

Eastern Michigan University

College of Human Services
Ypsilanti, MI 48197
Janet Boyd, Chairperson, Gerontology

The minor in gerontology is designed to
provide knowledge of the factors and problems related to the aging person. The minor

is not conceived as preparation for a specific career but, by coupling it with a major in one of the human service areas—e.g., social work, home economics, nursing, or occupational therapy—a student can enhance his or her major with this extra dimension of proficiency.

Minnesota
University of Minnesota
All-University Center on Aging
117 Pleasant Street, S.E.
Minneapolis, MN 55455
Donald G. McTavish and Frank M.
Lassman, Co-Chairpersons

The University of Minnesota offers a certificate in aging, designed to train persons already working with the elderly or those seeking to do so. The courses are offered at night through the General Extension program.

An undergraduate degree in gerontology is also offered. This may be obtained through several vehicles—the Bachelor of Applied Studies from the General College; Bachelor of Individualized Studies through the College of Liberal Arts; and the Inter-College Program through the University College. All three are individualized courses of study: the student would put together a multidisciplinary gerontology degree.

On the graduate level, specific gerontology degrees are offered through Long-Term Health Care Administration and the Geriatric Nurse Practitioner Program. It is also possible to have a gerontology focus in graduate programs such as sociology, social work, psychology, and public health.

Missouri
Washington University
Department of Psychology, Aging and
Development Program
St. Louis, MO 63130
Jack Botwinick, Director

A Ph.D. is offered in psychology with the opportunity to specialize in the psychology of aging. The emphasis is on training for a career in research and teaching.

Although there is a formal reciprocal arrangement between St. Louis University and Washington University, the emphasis of the two schools' programs is quite different: Washington University's focus is on research and St. Louis University's is a certificate program and is geared to service providers.

St. Louis University
Institute of Applied Gerontology
St. Louis, MO 63103
William J. Hutchinson, Director

The certificate of gerontology for fifteen credits can be applied to any graduate degree program or can be taken independently. The university also offers an undergraduate certificate in gerontology through its Metropolitan College.

University of Missouri
Center for Aging Studies
Columbia, MO 65201
Lee J. Cary, Director

The Center for Aging Studies' purpose is to help prepare people for gerontological careers. In addition, the center assists academic departments in developing new courses and new resources in aging and helps integrate the university's present resources in aging related activities.

Nebraska
University of Nebraska at Omaha
Gerontology Program
Omaha, NE 68101
David A. Peterson, Director

The gerontology program offers a certificate of specialization at undergraduate and graduate levels. Courses are generally offered in late afternoon or evening.

New Jersey
Rutgers — The State University
Intra-University Program in
Gerontology
4 Huntington Street
New Brunswick, NJ 08903
Marsel A. Heisel, Curriculum Specialist

The gerontology program is the response of Rutgers, The State University, to the need for gerontological education, research, training, and community service. The goal of the program is to serve the entire state of New Jersey with its numerous and diversified populations of older persons.

Innate in the gerontology program philosophy is a strong tie between the university and the community. The program is developing university/community gerontology education sites that will function as areas for education, research, and services, and where academicians, practitioners, and seniors may meet and exchange their insights and knowledge.

New York
State University of New York at Albany
School of Social Welfare
Institute of Gerontology
1400 Washington Avenue
Albany, NY 12222
Susan R. Sherman, Director

The Institute of Gerontology is a regional multidisciplinary gerontology center dedicated to research, education, and service. Associates of the institute, from a wide variety of academic departments and schools, participate in joint research projects. The institute also serves as an information clearing-house and a referral agency.

Institute associates teach a variety of on-campus courses related to aging. Additional programs include pre-retirement training; continuing education programs to area service personnel; training programs in adult services for staff of local departments of social services; and training of nursing home patient ombudsmen.

Associates of the institute participate in many activities to promote general awareness of gerontology, such as testifying before the legislature, participating in local and campus task forces, and providing speakers and organizing conferences for community and professional groups.

Syracuse University
All-University Gerontology Center
Syracuse, NY 13210
Walter M. Beattie, Jr., Director

The All-University Gerontology Center is located in a building complex that includes a public housing facility for older persons. The Certificate in Gerontology is awarded in connection with regular undergraduate and graduate degree programs. Many research projects are underway.

Elmira College
Aging Services
Elmira, NY 14901
Barbara L. Smith

Aging Services is a specialization under Human Services, leading to the bachelor's degree. Paraprofessionals may also earn a certificate in the field. A popular program for adults returning to college is a series of mini-workshops, which cover a variety of topics in a short period of time.

The Father of Gerontology

After he retired, V. Korenchevsky, a Russian-born doctor and physiologist, turned to the study of aging. He spent his retirement years advancing research in gerontology throughout the world and was the man primarily responsible for organizing the first International Gerontological Congress, in 1950.

St. Thomas Aquinas College
Institute on Aging
Sparkill, NY 10976
Dr. Mary A. Heffernan, Director

The college sponsors an annual six-day institute on aging and new trends in gerontology, in cooperation with Seton Hall University. Within the regular college program, a student may major in gerontology, leading to a bachelor of science degree.

Hunter College
Brookdale Center on Aging
129 E. 79th Street
New York, NY 10021
Rose Dobrof, Director

Supported by grants from the Brookdale Foundation, the Administration on Aging, and other foundations and public agencies, the Brookdale Center on Aging has developed courses and field work in training in Hunter's schools of social work, nursing, and allied health sciences and in departments of home economics, education, urban planning, and sociology.

Marymount Manhattan College
221 East 71 Street
New York, NY 10021

Gerontology is a program leading to a bachelor's degree in either psychology or sociology. Marymount grants credit for nontraditional learning activities, such as life-work experience.

Yeshiva University Gerontological Institute
Brookdale Center
55 Fifth Avenue
New York, NY 10003
Dr. Celia B. Weisman, Director

The Institute offers a post-master's certificate in gerontological practice. The program is aimed at professionals in social work, psychology, counseling, nursing, nursing home administration, rehabilitation, public health, the clergy, and related disciplines. It is designed both for those who are already working with the aging

and those who are considering a career in gerontology. Classes are held in the late afternoon and early evening.

New School for Social Research
Center for New York City Affairs
66 Fifth Avenue
New York, NY 10011
Henry Cohen, Dean

The New School offers a master of professional studies in gerontological services administration degree. All courses for students working in the field are scheduled for late afternoon, evening, or Saturdays. A separate day program is offered for students wishing to prepare to enter the field.

Adelphi University
Multidisciplinary Center on Aging
Garden City, NY 11530
Elaine B. Jacks, Director

The center has a variety of programs, including a Post-Baccalaureate Certificate in Gerontological Studies. Under contract with five New York counties and the State of Pennsylvania, the center offers multidisciplinary continuing education courses for professionals and paraprofessionals working with older persons. Workshops are held, and the center is developing employment/retirement programming and a resource center. Publications include *A Guide to Funding Sources in Aging* (see page 84) and *Finding a Job: A Resource Book for the Middle-Aged and Retired.*

Molloy College
Institute of Gerontology
Rockville Centre, NY 11570
Anne M. McIver, Director

The Institute of Gerontology is the sponsoring agent for seminars and workshops involved in the field of aging. The institute will afford those engaged, or who wish to become engaged, in the areas of human services an opportunity to update their credentials and/or earn college credit. Seminars and workshops are open to gerontology majors in order to enrich their program and to help them bridge the gap between "academia" and the "real world."

There is also a bachelor of arts degree program in gerontology offered as a single discipline with equal status as departments with other disciplines.

North Carolina
Duke University
Center for the Study of Aging and
  Human Development
Durham, NC 27710
George L. Maddox, Director

The Center for the Study of Aging and Human Development has cooperative programs of research, training, and service with the Law School, its family medicine program, and its new Center for Lifetime Learning. One of the oldest institutes on aging, Duke has a KWIC (Key-Word Indexed Collection) of documents, books, training manuals and materials, audio-visual resources, and other materials related to training resources in aging. For information about KWIC, write or phone Joan Walter at the center: 919-684-3058.

Ohio
Case Western Reserve University
Cleveland, OH 44106
James G. Taafe, Vice-President

In 1976, the university conducted a detailed, university-wide survey, itemizing a wide array of teaching, research, and advocacy activities in aging. These activities have not been centralized or coordinated, although exploration is continuing on how to focus what the university expects to be a major new emphasis in many of its programs and curricula.

Important specializations in aging are available to students in the professional degree programs in nursing and in social work, and an Office of Geriatric Medicine is currently being organized.

Kent State University
Interdisciplinary Council on Gerontology
Kent, OH 44242
Dorothy Fruit, Co-Chairperson

The bachelor of arts degree in gerontology is available through a consortium of thirteen departments in which persons may prepare themselves for a career in gerontology. This is administered through the School of Home Economics and offered as Option II, Gerontology, under Individual and Family Development.

Miami University
Scripps Foundation Gerontology Center
Oxford, OH 45056
Robert C. Atchley, Director

The center serves as a clearing-house for the university's educational programs, research, and public service in aging. Master's degree and undergraduate educational programs are offered in social gerontology.

Bowling Green University
Gerontology Degree Program
Bowling Green, OH 43403
John Hiltner, Director

The bachelor of science degree in gerontology is offered through the College of Health and Community Services. Many of the courses on aging are scheduled for late afternoon or evening.

University of Akron
Institute for Life-Span Development and
  Gerontology
Akron, OH 44325
Harvey L. Sterns, Director

In September 1978, the university inaugurated a certificate program in Life-Span Development: Adulthood and Aging, at the baccalaureate level. Upon successful completion of the requirements, students will be awarded this certificate when they receive a bachelor's degree in a chosen discipline.

The institute also conducts research, training, and community service programs.

Oregon
University of Oregon
Center for Gerontology
Eugene, OR 97403
Frances G. Scott, Director

The Center for Gerontology offers a multidisciplinary program. The university plans to begin offering the bachelor's and master's degrees in gerontology in fall 1979, as well as a certificate in gerontology designed for Continuing Education students. Persons 65 or older who are not seeking credit or not working toward a degree may attend classes free on a space-available basis, and are encouraged to do so. Retired persons from the university vicinity are given opportunities to serve as volunteers working with gerontology students on an individual basis, thus contributing to the student's education and knowledge of the aging process.

Oregon State University

Program on Gerontology
Family Life Department
Corvallis, OR 97331
Vicki L. Schmall, Director

The Program on Gerontology is multidisciplinary, with courses offered by several academic departments. The program is directed toward students planning to pursue a career in aging and those with an interest in other professional areas. Traineeships are available to both undergraduate and graduate students who plan to work with older adults.

In addition to courses in gerontology, community field practicums are available to students. Concurrent enrollment policies of Oregon State enable students to take courses in gerontology at Portland State University and the University of Oregon.

Other learning opportunities, such as research projects, community workshops, and grant writing, are available to students. Conferences led by prominent professionals are also held, and students are given the opportunity to facilitate conference sessions.

A Health Care Administration Program is also offered, through the schools of business, health and physical education, and home economics.

Portland State University

Institute on Aging
Multidisciplinary Center of Gerontology
Portland, OR 97207
Douglas G. Montgomery, Acting Director

Located within the School of Urban Affairs, the Institute on Aging coordinates the research, training, and service functions of the university that bear on the broad issues of adult development and human aging. Although each project or activity of the institute is primarily designed for service, training, or research, each is also intended to provide an involvement of all three dimensions.

Multidisciplinary center status came with the award of a grant from the Administration on Aging in 1977. With this grant the institute can further develop its certificate program in gerontology. The funds are being used to supplement and expand the areas of curriculum and training, research, and community service.

Pennsylvania
Pennsylvania State University

Gerontology Center
University Park, PA 16802
Joseph H. Britton, Chairman

The purpose of the center is to promote the study of aging; to stimulate communication among scholars, practitioners, officials, and others; to expand education and training in aging; and to foster application of research in the field. Some ninety "Faculty Affiliates in Gerontology" participate in teaching, research, and service projects throughout the university. A Gerontological Resource Center and a Sociological Archive of General Studies in Aging are resources for training and research.

Tennessee
Fisk University

Program in Social Gerontology
Nashville, TN 37203
Carroll J. Bourg, Director of Graduate Training

A two-year program leads to a master of arts in social gerontology degree. Courses are usually arranged in the late afternoon. Part-time students are welcomed.

Texas

North Texas State University
Center for Studies in Aging
Denton, TX 76203
Hiram J. Friedsam and Cora A. Martin, Co-Directors

The Center for Studies in Aging, established in 1967, was one of the first to offer a master's degree in aging studies. Graduates—more than 90 percent of whom remain in work directly connected to the elderly—find employment in long-term case administration; retirement housing; federal, state, and local agencies; adult education; senior centers; mental health programs; industrial retirement programs; adult counseling; and recreation work.

North Texas State also offers a certificate program for graduate students and a minor in aging studies at both the graduate and undergraduate levels. In 1974, the center began a program to meet the needs of practitioners in the field who wanted to take formal courses in gerontology without taking extended leave from their jobs. Summer institutes consist of four two-week intensive sessions, arranged so that the requirements for the master's degree can be completed in five years.

Trinity University
Center for Research and Training in Gerontology
715 Stadium Drive
San Antonio, TX 78284
David Oliver, Director

The Center for Research and Training in Gerontology offers a basic course of study leading to a master of arts degree in gerontology with specialized tracks for students interested in pursuing one of the following career options: social services; public policy and planning; long-term health care; or preparation for further graduate work.

Utah

University of Utah
Rocky Mountain Gerontology Center
2034 Annex Building
Salt Lake City, UT 84112
Melvin A. White, Director

The Rocky Mountain Gerontology Center is one of the nation's largest gerontological consortia with five member institutions including Brigham Young University, Southern Utah State College, University of Utah, Utah State University, and Weber State College. The center is involved in both multidisciplinary research and training in the field of aging. Both an undergraduate and graduate certificate in gerontology are offered, as well as a certificate of completion (for practitioners). Field work is a major part of the undergraduate and graduate programs. Course work is multidisciplinary.

Virginia

Virginia Commonwealth University
Virginia Center on Aging
Richmond, VA 23284
Greg Arling, Director

The Virginia Commonwealth University offers a master of science degree in gerontology through its gerontology program. Graduate and undergraduate students may also take courses in aging from various departments on the academic and medical college campuses. The university administers the Virginia Center on Aging, a state multidisciplinary center for gerontological research and education. Through its programs, schools, and departments, the university has a full range of activities in education, research, and community service for aging.

Washington

University of Washington
Institute on Aging
Seattle, WA 98195
Alice J. Kethley, Acting Associate Director

After almost a decade of development, the Institute on Aging was formally established in late 1977. The institute, a multidisciplinary program involving twelve schools and colleges at the university, has the goal of providing Washington State and the Pacific Northwest with a university-based gerontological training and research center.

Central Washington State College

Studies toward Aging and Retirement
Ellensburg, WA 98926
Elwyn H. Odell, Coordinator

Studies toward Aging and Retirement offers an interdisciplinary major in gerontology for the B.A. (interdepartmental major), and the M.A. (individualized study major). The program is designed for those who seek careers in the field of aging, and also provides in-service training for those already in the profession.

West Virginia

West Virginia University

Department of Psychology
Morgantown, WV 26506
Nancy Datan

The university offers a Ph.D. in life-span developmental psychology with research concentration in aging.

The Career Training Project for Work with Elderly People is offered through the School of Social Work. The program leads to a master's degree in social work with special preparation for careers in planning, developing, and managing services for the elderly. There are a limited number of required courses and a wide range of electives, from which it is possible to put together a specialization in gerontology. The program also includes field work.

Funds are available for tuition, fees, and stipends for students who can establish financial need.

Wisconsin

University of Wisconsin

Faye McBeath Institute on Aging and
Adult Life

425 Henry Mall
Madison, WI 53706
Martin B. Loeb, Director

The University of Wisconsin offers courses and programs through many of its schools and departments: continuing and vocational education, economics, educational psychology, law, library science, nursing, occupational therapy, philosophy, physical education, medicine, social work, and sociology.

Although the Faye McBeath Institute does not, itself, offer courses or grant degrees, it publicizes the courses offered on campus and promotes new offerings in response to identified needs. It also brings together students from all of the disciplines and professions throughout the university in a student organization. One of the institute's major functions is to facilitate interdisciplinary research projects. Another is to help apply the research information developed at the university to community organizations and the state, and to work actively with local and state agencies through its community service program.

CHAPTER 12

Organizations

Government Agencies and Committees

Administration on Aging

Department of Health, Education and Welfare
Washington, DC 20201
Robert Benedict, Commissioner

This is the major administrative body in the federal government concerned with aging. On the local level, the AOA works through state offices (see appendix) and more than 500 Area Offices on Aging.

National Institute on Aging

National Institutes of Health
Department of Health, Education and Welfare
Bethesda, MD 20014
Dr. Robert N. Butler, Director

NIA, the youngest and smallest of the eleven National Institutes of Health, came into being in 1975. Its director, Dr. Butler, a psychiatrist, is the author of the Pulitzer-Prize-winning book, *Why Survive? Being Old in America*. NIA is the research arm of the federal government and, unlike the Administration on Aging, does not deal with the actual delivery of services, even health services, except as it can provide fundamental information on which to base decisions.

(For a description of the research programs of NIA, see chapter 10.)

Special Committee on Aging

U.S. Senate
Washington, DC 20510
Senator Frank Church, Chairman

Select Committee on Aging

U.S. House of Representatives
Washington, DC 20515
Rep. Claude Pepper, Chairman

Nonprofit Organizations

The National Council on the Aging, Inc.

1828 L Street, N.W.
Washington, DC 20036
202-223-6250

The National Council on the Aging is a nonprofit, membership organization of professionals, organizations, and the concerned public. Since its inception in 1950, it has worked to improve the lives of older Americans by helping to eliminate problems of aging and opening up opportunities for older people.

Although it operates in a number of areas, one of the most interesting of the current ones is the National Media Resource Center on Aging. This is the focus of the first nationwide effort to change negative perceptions of older people. The MRC funded the Louis Harris study in 1975, *The Myth and Reality of Aging in America,* an intensive nationwide survey of America's attitudes toward aging and the aged. This survey, which is required reading for almost anyone interested in the field, has served as a base for the Media Resource Center's activities, which are to enable older people to participate more fully in the job market, volunteer services, and community activities. The Media Resource Center supplies information to editors, writers, producers, filmmakers, and others to help them project a more accurate image of the elderly.

Other areas of activity of the NCOA are the National Institute of Senior Centers; the Senior Center Humanities Program (see pages 95–96); the National Institute of Work and Retirement; the Pre-Retirement Planning Project; the NCOA Housing Corporation; the National Voluntary Organizations for Independent Living for the Aging; the Public Policy Center; the Center on Arts and the Aging, and an Intergenerational Services Program.

The National Council on the Aging maintains the largest, most comprehensive library in the nation devoted to the field of aging. It also has produced and published more than one hundred books and pamphlets. A publications list is available.

National Senior Citizen's Law Center
Main Office
1709 W. 8th Street
Los Angeles, CA 90017
213-483-3990
Branch Office
1200 15th Street, N.W.
Washington, DC 20005
202-872-1404

The National Senior Citizen's Law Center is funded by the Legal Services Corporation of the Department of Justice and HEW's Administration on Aging. It provides technical assistance in cases involving the elderly, including acting as co-counsel or providing expert testimony. It acts as a clearing-house of information in such areas as social security, private and public pensions, Medicare and Medicaid, age discrimination and mandatory retirement, consumer and housing problems, and older women's problems. It has published numerous materials and maintains files on court pleadings, administrative rulings, etc.

A major NSCLC activity is to help expand high-quality legal services for the elderly, working with legal services programs and Area Offices on Aging.

The National Caucus on the Black Aged
and
The National Center on the Black Aged
1424 K Street, N.W.
Washington, DC 20005

The National Caucus on the Black Aged was founded in 1970 as an advocacy organization to address the critical concerns and special needs of aging and aged blacks at the 1971 White House Conference on Aging. The caucus is a membership organization that advocates adequate income, health, and housing for the black aged. Members include black seniors, community leaders, social scientists, and aging specialists from across the United States. The caucus has a growing network of local chapters that address the socioeconomic needs and welfare of aging and aged blacks.

The National Center on the Black Aged was established by the National Caucus on the Black Aged, as a nonprofit, private organization. The center provides technical assistance to members of the caucus and works with both public and private organizations to improve policies, programs, and delivery of services to black and low-income elderly. Its main activities include research, technical and training assistance, curriculum and legislative development, dissemination of information, and promotion of blacks in careers in the field of aging.

The center has initiated a Job Bank Service as a means of introducing black professionals and paraprofessionals in the field of gerontology to employers seeking qualified personnel.

The job bank will be a repository for information about positions currently available in the field of aging, and for the qualifications and backgrounds of persons seeking employment. Applications will be screened and those that match specified job descriptions will be forwarded to employers.

As a special feature, the service includes assistance in the placement of older persons seeking part-time, paid employment, or volunteer positions in the field of aging.

The service is free to members of the organization. Prospective job candidates who are not members of NCBA are charged $2.00 to cover postage fees for one year from the date of registration. Further information is available from Elizabeth A. Brooks, Personnel Coordinator for the center.

American Association of Retired Persons (AARP) and National Retired Teachers Association (NRTA)

1909 K Street, N.W.
Washington, DC 20049

When you consider that the AARP's parent organization, NRTA, was founded by a schoolteacher, Ethel Percy Andrus, who couldn't get insurance after she retired, this has to be the ultimate success story. Insurance is what has brought millions of members into AARP—and many more millions of dollars to the Colonial Penn Insurance companies.

I find it difficult to write about the AARP. On the one hand, with 11 million members it is the largest and therefore one of the most important of the organizations of older people. More than that, though, it provides, supports, and funds many excellent services and programs for all older people, not just its members. Some of them have been described in this book.

On the other hand, it is impossible not to feel uncomfortable about the close relationship between AARP and the Colonial Penn Group, which not only has a monopoly on all AARP insurance, but owns the AARP travel service and Mature Temps, the employment agency recommended by AARP. These companies prepare the ads— they look more like articles—that appear in the organization's newsletters and magazines. Members receive insurance solicitations, not only from Colonial Penn (which has to pay regular postage) but from AARP, which has a nonprofit postage permit. Colonial Penn not only saves three fourths of the cost of postage, their solicitations come from the president of the AARP.

How much the policies of AARP have been affected by its relationship with a commercial insurance company is open to speculation. To my knowledge, AARP has never been accused of improprieties because of this arrangement, although the Postal Service has been investigating the use of the nonprofit postal rate for an insurance company's pitch.

If AARP once needed the insurance company's subsidy, with 11 million members it surely doesn't need it now. It seems too bad that any cloud should hang over such a useful, important organization in the field of aging.

Membership dues in AARP are $3 a year. Benefits include discounts on drugs—the AARP has its own pharmacies in seven cities, which also fill mail orders—and discounts on hotels, motels, and car rentals. There are 2800 local chapters.

The AARP's Generations Alliance program brings local groups of older and younger people together for discussions and such community service activities as tree planting and city beautification projects. *Photo credit: AARP*

National Council of Senior Citizens

1511 K Street, N.W.
Washington, DC 20005
202-783-6850

A membership organization of 3.5 million in 3800 clubs nationwide, the NCSC describes itself as "nonprofit, nonpartisan, but definitely *not* nonpolitical." Indeed, the NCSC is an extremely political body, having got its start in the fight over Medicare in the early 1960s. Originally funded by labor unions and comprised primarily of union members, the NCSC has in recent years attracted a large enough membership (anyone of any age may join) to become less dependent on union funding.

Although it is politically active for the benefit of older people, the NCSC has also backed legislation in other areas—the 1971 child-care bill, the lowering of the voting age to 18, clean air and water legislation, legal protection for the consumer, and other similar measures.

In addition to its political activities, the NCSC offers members group health insurance, discounts on drugs, motels, and car rentals, and group travel plans. The annual dues of $4 for an individual member or $3.50 for those enrolling through an affiliated club or supporting union, include a subscription to the council's newsletter, *Senior Citizens News.* Once a year the paper prints congressmen's voting records on legislation affecting the elderly.

National Association of Retired Federal Employees

1533 New Hampshire Avenue, N.W.
Washington, DC 20036

NARFE is exclusively concerned with representing the interests of all persons qualified under the federal government's retirement programs.

Founded in 1921, NARFE sponsored the enactment of the legislation that today constitutes the federal civilian retirement system. NARFE monitors all legislative proposals coming before Congress and state legislatures that may affect the interests of NARFE members in other areas such as health care, taxes, and consumer protection.

NARFE has local chapters that provide recreational, social, and community activities. The organization is becoming involved in pre-retirement counseling, and members participate as speakers and panel discussion leaders in pre-retirement seminars.

National Association of Mature People

2000 Classen Center
P.O. Box 26792
Oklahoma City, OK 73126
405-523-2060

A membership organization of approximately 140 thousand people over 55, NAMP offers group insurance, travel programs, discount drugs, and other services. The membership fee of $4 a year includes a subscription to their magazine, *Best Years* and to *NAMP News.*

The Gray Panthers

3700 Chestnut Street
Philadelphia, PA 19104
215-382-6644

See chapter 3 for a full discussion of this organization.

Older Women's Rights Committee

3800 Harrison Street
Oakland, CA 94611
Tish Sommers, Coordinator

Since 1974, the National Organization for Women (NOW) has had a Task Force on Older Women, which functions with considerable autonomy. When all of the NOW task forces were abolished and replaced with broad standing committees covering the issues of concern to NOW, this became one of them. The committee will continue to promote the rights of older women, both within and outside the NOW organization.

Appendix

State Offices on Aging

Alabama
Commission on Aging
  740 Madison Avenue
  Montgomery, AL 36104
  205-832-6640
  Emmett W. Eaton, Executive Director

Alaska
Office on Aging
  Pouch H-OIC
  Juneau, AK 99811
  907-586-6153
  Dan Plotnick, Coordinator

Arizona
Bureau on Aging
  Department of Economic Security
  111 W. Osborn Road
  Phoenix, AZ 85013
  602-271-4446

Arkansas
Office on Aging
  West Park Building, No. 2
  7107 W. 12th Street
  Little Rock, AR 72203
  501-371-2441
  Phil S. Peters, Director

California
Department of Aging
  918 J Street
  Sacramento, CA 95814
  916-322-2887
  Janet J. Levy, Director

Colorado
Division of Services for the Aging
  Department of Social Services
  1575 Sherman Street
  Denver, CO 80203
  303-892-2651
  Dorothy Anders, Director

Connecticut
Department on Aging
  90 Washington Street, Room 312
  Hartford, CT 06115
  203-566-2480
  William R. Ratchford, Commissioner

Delaware
Division of Aging
  Department of Health and Social
    Services
  New Castle, DE 19720
  302-421-6791

District of Columbia
Division of Services to the Aged
  Munsey Building
  1329 E Street, N.W.
  Washington, DC 20009
  202-638-2406

Florida
Aging and Adult Services Program Office
  1321 Winewood Boulevard
  Tallahassee, FL 32301
  904-488-2650
  E. Bentley Lipscomb, Director

Georgia
Office of Aging
  Department of Human Resources
  47 Trinity Avenue
  Atlanta, GA 30308
  404-894-5333

Hawaii
Executive Office on Aging
  Office of the Governor
  1149 Bethel Street, Room 307
  Honolulu, HI 96813
  808-548-2593

Idaho
Office on Aging
  State House
  Boise, ID 83720
  208-384-3833
  John M. McCullen, Director

Illinois
Department on Aging
  421 E. Capitol Avenue
  Springfield, IL 62706
  217-782-5773

Indiana
Commission on the Aging and the Aged
  215 N. Senate Avenue, Room 201
  Indianapolis, IN 46202
  317-633-5948
  Maurice E. Endwright, Executive
    Director

Iowa
Commission on the Aging
  415 Tenth Street
  Des Moines, IA 50319
  515-281-5187
  Glenn Bowles, Executive Director

Kansas
Department on Aging
  State Office Building
  Topeka, KS 66612
  913-296-4986
  Forrest J. Robinson, Secretary

Kentucky
Department for Human Resources
  Center for Aging Services
  275 E. Main Street
  Frankfort, KY 40601
  502-564-6930
  Sam Jones, Director

Louisiana
Bureau of Aging Services
  Office of Human Resources
  P.O. Box 44282
  Baton Rouge, LA 70804
  504-389-2172

Maine
Bureau of Maine's Elderly
  Department of Human Services
  State House
  Augusta, ME 04333
  207-289-2561
  Richard Michaud, Director

Maryland
Office on Aging
  State Office Building, Room 1004
  301 W. Preston Street
  Baltimore, MD 21201
  301-383-2100
  Matthew Tayback, Director

Massachusetts
Department of Elder Affairs
110 Tremont Street
Boston, MA 02108
617-727-7750
James J. Callahan, Jr., Secretary

Michigan
Office of Services to the Aging
300 Michigan Avenue
Lansing, MI 48909
517-373-8230
Elizabeth Ferguson, Director

Minnesota
Minnesota Board on Aging
Metro Square Building, Suite 204
7th and Roberts Streets
St. Paul, MN 55101
612-296-2770
Gerald A. Bloedow, Executive Secretary

Mississippi
Council on Aging
510 George Street
Jackson, MS 39216
601-354-6590
Norman Harris, Executive Director

Missouri
Office of Aging
Department of Social Services
Broadway State Office Building
Jefferson City, MO 65101
314-751-2075
E. C. Walker, Director

Montana
Aging Service Bureau
Department of Social and Rehabilitative
  Services
Helena, MT 59601
406-449-3124

Nebraska
Commission on Aging
301 Centennial Mall S.

Lincoln, NE 68509
402-471-2306
David Howard, Executive Director

Nevada
Division of Aging
Department of Human Resources
505 E. King Street
Carson City, NV 89701
702-885-4210
John B. McSweeney, Administrator

New Hampshire
Council on Aging
14 Depot Street
Concord, NH 03301
603-271-2751
Claira P. Monier, Director

New Jersey
Division on Aging
Department of Community Affairs
363 W. State Street
Trenton, NJ 08625
609-292-3765
James J. Pennestri, Director

New Mexico
State Commission on Aging
408 Galisteo Street
Santa Fe, NM 87503
505-827-5258
G. Randy Romero, Director

New York
Office for the Aging
Agency Building 2
Empire State Plaza
Albany, NY 12223
Mrs. Tom Glasse, Director

New York City
State Office for the Aging
2 World Trade Center, Room 5036
New York, NY 10047
212-488-6405
Harold Scher, Administrator

North Carolina
Division of Aging
  Department of Human Resources
  213 Hillsborough Street
  Raleigh, NC 27603
  919-733-3983
  Nathan H. Yelton, Assistant Secretary

North Dakota
Aging Services Unit
  Social Service Board of North Dakota
  State Capitol Building
  Bismarck, ND 58505
  701-224-2577
  G. D. Shaw, Administrator

Ohio
Commission on Aging
  50 W. Broad Street
  Columbus, OH 43215
  614-466-5500
  Martin A. Janis, Director

Oklahoma
Special Unit on Aging
  Department of Institutions, Social and
    Rehabilitative Services
  Oklahoma City, OK 73125
  405-521-2281
  Roy R. Keen, Supervisor

Oregon
Office of Elderly Affairs
  772 Commercial Street, S.E.
  Salem, OR 97310
  503-378-4728
  Marvin Janzen, Administrator

Pennsylvania
Office for the Aging
  Department of Public Welfare
  510 Health and Welfare Building
  Harrisburg, PA 17120
  717-787-5350

Rhode Island
Department of Elderly Affairs
  150 Washington Street

  Providence, RI 02903
  401-277-2858
  Anna M. Tucker, Director

South Carolina
Commission on Aging
  915 Main Street
  Columbia, SC 29201
  803-758-2576
  Harry R. Bryan, Director

South Dakota
Office on Aging
  Department of Social Services
  State Office Building
  Pierre, SD 57501
  605-224-3656
  James V. Anderson, Administrator

Tennessee
Commission on Aging
  306 Gay Street
  Nashville, TN 37201
  615-741-2056
  Tom Henry, Executive Director

Texas
Governor's Committee on Aging
  411 W. 13th Street
  Austin, TX 78711
  512-475-2717
  Vernon McDaniel, Executive Director

Utah
State Division of Aging
  150 W. North Temple
  Salt Lake City, UT 84103
  801-533-6422
  F. Leon Povey, Director

Vermont
Office on Aging
  State Office Building
  Montpelier, VT 05602
  802-244-5181, ext. 400
  Pearl B. Somaini-Dayer, Director

Virginia
Office on Aging
830 E. Main Street, Suite 950
Richmond, VA 23219
804-786-7894
Edwin L. Wood, Director

Washington
Office on Aging
Department of Social and Health
Services
Olympia, WA 98504
206-753-2502
Charles Reed, Chief

West Virginia
Commission on Aging
State Capitol
Charleston, WV 25305
304-348-3317
Louise B. Gerrard, Executive Director

Wisconsin
Bureau of Aging
Department of Health and Social
Services
1 W. Wilson Street, Room 700
Madison, WI 53702
608-266-2536
Douglas Nelson, Director

Wyoming
Aging Services
Division of Public Assistance and Social
Services
State Office Building, W.
Cheyenne, WY 82002
307-777-7561